I0511200

Table of Contents

Summary

Acknowledgments

About the presentations

Conclusion

Sources of data

The author

ISBN-13:
978-1541157231

ISBN-10:
1541157230

Summary

I have been a student of healthcare for much of my professional life. This industry, which reflects our society's priorities, is different in its essence from others whose focus is to *improve* production and our quality of life.

My industry, that is healthcare, deals with the well-being we believe to be a requisite, or gateway, to improve everything else.

The healthcare industry has been a powerful mentor since the day, 28 years ago, that I started listening and noticed a need for a "bottom-up," approach for organization-wide change.

I applied the organization-wide, "bottom-up" approach practiced at manufacturing and service industries, to the healthcare industry to make it more effective and efficient. Two hundred and fifty projects later, the organizations that adopted this approach have realized annual cost reductions averaging 9 percent annually without negative impact on patient care, and a 9- to 24-year sustainable results. It became the standard approach followed by others.

The "bottom-up" approach established a need for data-driven national hospital scorecard, where none existed. The result was the joint creation, with a data firm, of the *"100 Top Hospitals"* study. It was not an initiative well-received, at first, in the industry by those who didn't make it to the *Top 100*.   What has followed is predictable: The study is now in its 23rd year and going strong. Some Board of Trustees now incorporate achieving the *Top 100* as a goal for CEOs.

The same thing happened when, noting another void in the industry, I co-founded *Performance Logic*, a company that would embed hospital cost-reduction into a knowledge-based software system. Such a self-help tool would help in redesigning operations. Once clients started to use the tool, it morphed into something else – project and portfolio management. *Performance Logic* fulfills that need to this day.

It is this listening that became a career. Today, hundreds of studies and thousands of employees later, I can tell you that what works with Group A will work with Group Z.

Data-driven? Bottom-up? The terms are deceptively simple. Could these concepts actually hold the secret to analyzing an entire industry? Yes. In fact, if we are ready to listen, the terms provide the solution to any problem-solving in the public, private and non-profit entity.

Where does one start with these concepts?

What is needed is basic:

- Teams of employees ready to make good-faith efforts to reduce costs or expand duties
- A chief-executive-officer who commits to implementing those changes.

That's it. Welcome to what we call, "bottom-up."

What was clear at the onset of my work is even more-so today. What applies in healthcare has **applied to manufacturing and services. What applies to the private sector can be ported to the world of** non-profits. And, believe it or not, what applies with human beings in these groups does apply to *government*. Yes, it *does*. Even government. City, county, state, federal. Irrigation districts. Animal control shelters. Armed forces.

This was less an epiphany than a long seminar from those in every branch of the healthcare industry. And it led to the intersection of my personal and professional lives.

I am an Iraqi expatriate, a British and U.S. educated engineer and businessman, whose livelihood has been well outside of the political spheres occupied for decades by friends and family. Still, I remain connected to the land of my birth by family, professional endeavors and conviction. So, 12 years ago, when I was asked to give a presentation on what seem like the intractable problems of Iraq, I accepted the challenge with uncertainty, commitment and curiosity. "OK," I said to myself, "If I have been a diaspora critic of Iraq, what might I do to actually help problem-solve?". I prepared for the presentation armed with the knowledge of a country in turmoil and a professional track-record in management. How might I marry the two?

The Iraq presentation, made me realize that there was another new concept in the making – utilizing proven management practices for solving political problems. The concept would be no different: utilize teams of employees impacted by any change, to develop the recommendations to redesign the operation and organization ("bottom-up"). Arm them with data analyses, proven templates and processes, and they will deliver measurable outcomes.

Six presentations later, I see the need, once again, to spread the word via an educational service. These initial presentations covered issues that I consider paramount in 2016 --- healthcare, elections and the decline of civilizations, especially with an eye toward what can (not) be done to forestall that of the United States.

These presentations, Part 1, comprise the debut of *Grassroots Metamorphosis*.

There is more to come. How often do we hear about the impasses in national policy? How often do we decry the inaction of our electorate? How often do we wonder whether a decision to send troops abroad is prudent?

Are we really in search of a solution to what we have come to accept as inevitable gridlock? If we are ready to follow a *bottom-up* approach, then solutions are within our reach. Prepare to see it, soon, applied to a **community**, service or government branch near *you*.

Acknowledgements

Without the effort of a very capable team, this two-part book would not have been created. I thank them all for making this a quality "bottom-up," effort.

Keith Rosenblum, a friend, journalist and past communications director for Congressman Jim Kolbe, R-AZ, retired, helped me focus on the theme and title. He took dry, business-like style of writing and made it fun. He also interviewed colleagues to solicit perspectives of "bottom-up" management.

Barb Jardee, of Jardee Transcription, transcribed the audio from the presentation into notes that accompany each slide. Julia Denton edited the notes.

Kerry Trueman, of Anara Design, designed the covers.

The 20 plus individuals who reviewed the book draft and suggested changes.

Finally, the hundreds of individuals who attended the presentations, asked penetrating questions, challenged me and provided additional ideas and recommendations.

> **This book, in both parts, is dedicated to the individuals who attended the presentations over the past 12 years.**

The presentations

The presentations in this book provide the "bottom-up" approach for dealing with three of the seminal issues facing the United States:

1. **The decline of the United States over the past few decades, and how to reposition it**. The belief held by over 60 percent of citizens, that the country is heading in the wrong direction, is confirmed by many measures in this presentation. These same unhappy people are looking for ways they can help change the direction, as provided in the second presentation.

2. **Re-engineering Federal Elections**, as over 80 percent of the electorate is dissatisfied with the performance of Congress and want it more effective. The chapter provides helpful tools for the electorate to create "bottom-up" ways to improve elections outcome.

3. **Healthcare: Avoiding the crisis of an enabling industry**. Healthcare costs now exceed 17% of GDP and is growing. These costs are becoming a burden on citizens and putting pressure on businesses to compete in a global economy. This chapter provides a helpful strategy to mitigate the likely crises of the industry.

The presentations are the same offered different audiences over the past 12 years. Their purpose is to prompt audiences to ask questions and participate in developing practical solutions. They utilize data, analysis, proven template and structures, and logical arguments to suggest sound management solutions rather than those based on agendas or political viewpoints. They are intended to educate and challenge pre-conceived ideas.

All past presentations were interactive. The body of a presentation typically consumes half the time, with the other half allocated to extensive Q&A. Audience input is garnered regularly and is utilized in subsequent versions of the presentation to strengthen the argument.

The presentations draw virtually all data from primary research sources -- organizations that conduct the research directly. These include, the Central Intelligence Agency (CIA) World Factbook, Organization for Economic Co-operation and Development (OECD) United Nations and its entities, The World Bank, Fund for Peace, and Transparency International, among others. Books and special studies are utilized for medieval or prehistoric data and forecasts. A list of the data sources and books reviewed are included under *Sources of Data*.

This book was written in a format of **"text-plus-presentations,"** with notes elaborating each slide. You will need to review the presentations in sequence as the information in one presentation is relevant to a subsequent presentation.

Such has been the enthusiastic endorsement by the host groups that it has served as a catalyst for this initiative. See sample comments on the next page:

"Thunder Mountain Republican Women's Club of Sierra Vista, Arizona had the pleasure of having Sa'ad Allawi speak to our club in 2015 and 2016. Both of his presentations were excellent, well researched and VERY educational. The topics that we enjoyed were: "Anger in the Arab World and Re-Engineering Federal Elections". You would not go wrong in having him as a guest lecturer." **Leah Davis, Membership Chair, Thunder Mountain Republican Women**

"Mr. Sa'ad Allawi's presentations and courses were forward-looking, unconventional and topical; they lead to serious. thinking. I, generally, heard only interest and satisfaction with them to the Sun City Oro Valley community. In a couple of courses, Sa'ad took some risk in exposing his frank point of view about what he called the "decline of the U.S.A", while, constructively, suggesting ways to correct the situation" **Gaston Meloche, ILR – Sun City Vistoso**

"Like DE Tocqueville, Sa'ad Allawi is in a unique position to inspect and comment on American culture and our political system. Coming from Iraq originally but being in the United Sates for decades, Sa'ad's grasp of what made our country great is spot on and his opinions of where we got lost need to be heavily considered. If we understand our decline, then we can either try and slow or reverse the trend. His road map of how we need do just that is a must for many who are frustrated with the state of our Union today. **Jeff Utsch, - Heirs of the Republic**

"Management by facts and process. If you want to understand how to manage effectively review the Principles around process management as presented in this book. Mr. Allawi combines real world experience to help you understand how to effectively manage change"
A. Agarwal, Adjunct Professor - International Business, Eller College of Management

"Sa'ad has presented to our chapter of professionals on a number of occasions. His talks on Project and Project Portfolio Management have been well attended, and the feedback from participants has been excellent." **Kevin Archbold, Tucson Chapter of PMI**

The presentations are proprietary and cannot be used for copying, distribution or presentations. If you would like to do so, contact the author for permission and alternatives at sjallawi@gmail.com

Chapter 1
Empires, Civilizations and the United States

This presentation utilizes data to demonstrate that the United States is no different from any other empire or civilization that came before it – it is formed, grows, plateaus., and declines.

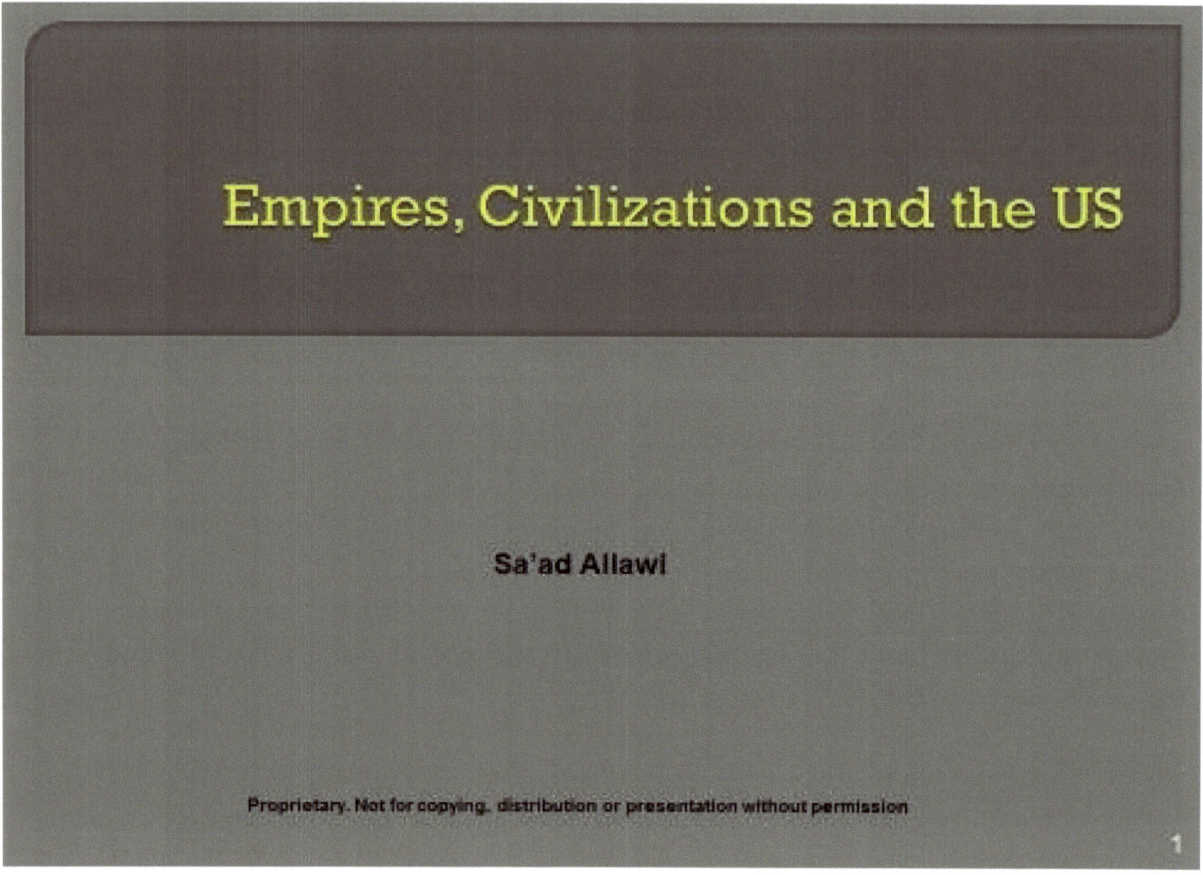

This presentation discusses the rise and decline of empires over time. It then discusses the absolute and relative decline of the U.S. over the past few decades in fiscal, economic, and social terms; hypothesizes the reasons for the decline; and highlights the two possible scenarios for repositioning the U.S.: slowing the decline or retrenching to a country. This presentation lays the groundwork for the following presentation to discuss the possible solutions.

While much of the discussion in this chapter and subsequent chapter relate to the U.S., many of the principles and items discussed apply equally to other western-style democracies, including European countries and Australia. The title of this particular chapter is Empires, Civilizations, and the U.S.

Publicly available sources are used for data regarding trends. Some sources have tracked results for 40 years or longer, while other sources have been tracking results for only two or three years. The trends utilized in this presentation are 25 years (one generation) or less, depending on the source.

Today's discussion covers three topics

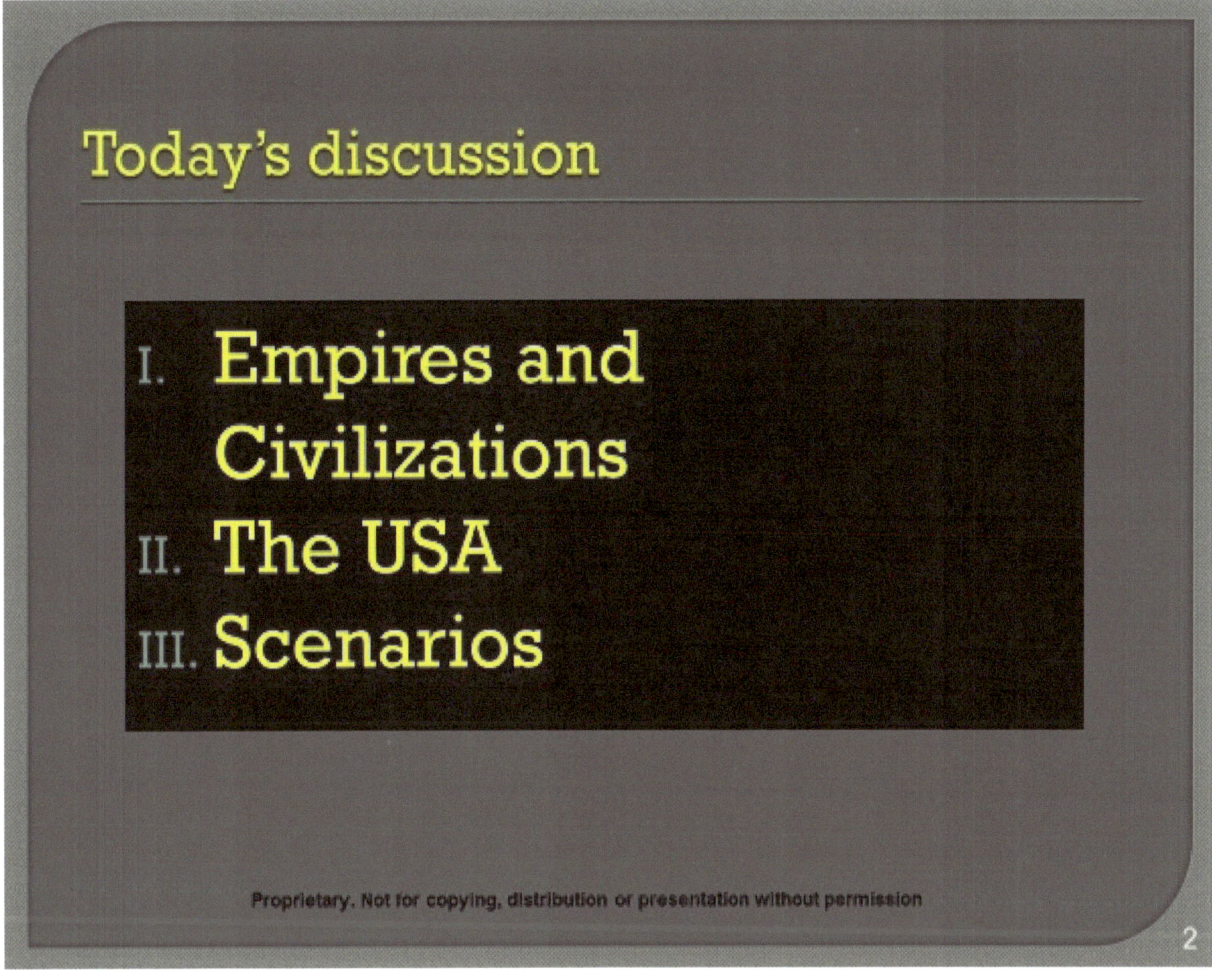

The evolution of empires and civilizations throughout history, the decline of the U.S. over the past few decades, and two possible scenarios for slowing the decline.

I. Empires – Comparisons

Empire/Civilization	Period (Approximate)	Approx. Length (Years)	% of world population at peak
Greek (Macedonian)	808 – 179 BC	629	40 (est.)
Persian*	658 BC – 651 AD	1309	35
Roman	27 BC – 1453 AD	1480	38
Islamic/Ottoman	632 – 1923	1291	23
Mongol	1206 – 1370	164	26
Spanish	1436 – 1808	372	12
Ming Dynasty	1368 - 1644	276	29
Qing Dynasty	1644 – 1912	268	37
Russian	1721 – 1917	196	10
British	1583 – 1997	414	20

* Achaemenes/Sassanid

Proprietary. Not for copying, distribution or presentation without permission

3

This chart shows a number of examples of empires and civilizations, listing the name of each empire, the approximate period during which it was an empire, and the approximate percent of population that empire/civilization controlled at its peak. These are a few randomly selected examples from a long list of empires and civilizations.

This group of examples starts with the Greeks and Macedonians and extends to the British Empire. The Greek Empire lasted for approximately 629 years (808 and 179 B.C.) and controlled about 40% of the world's population. The Islamic and Ottoman Empires lasted from 632 to 1923 (1,291 years) and controlled about 23% of the population. The Roman Empire lasted almost 1,500 years (27 B.C. to 1453 A.D.) and controlled approximately 38% of the world's population,

Some of the smaller civilizations, such as the Mongol Empire, lasted 164 years (1206 to 1370 A.D.) and controlled about 26% of the world's population,

The British Empire (which we'll discuss further on the next page) lasted 414 years and controlled about 20% of the world's population, with a very large footprint – 25% of the world's land.

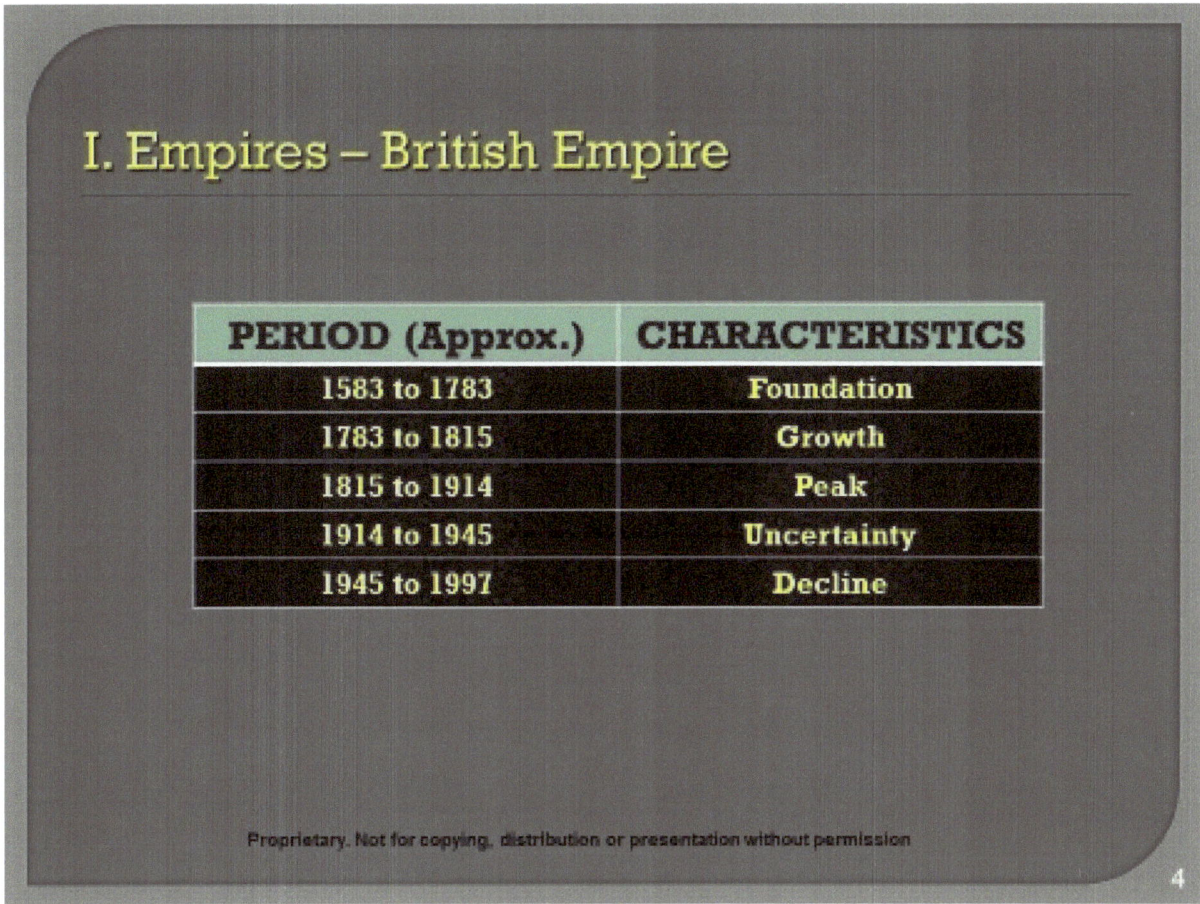

The British Empire had a number of periods (all dates are approximate):

- 1583 to 1783 marked the period of foundation.
- 1783 to 1815 was a period of growth.
- 1815 to 1914 was a period of peak.
- 1914 to 1945 was a period of uncertainty during the two World Wars.
- 1945 to 1997 represented a period of decline.

The British Empire ended officially in 1997 when the last colony, Hong Kong, was returned to the Chinese.

I. Empires – Life cycles of civilizations

- All entities are born, grow, decline and die
- This applies equally to organizations, civilizations and empire
- Historians, philosophers and sociologists have discussed this topic over the years *e.g. Spengler, Toynbee, Sorkin, Nisbet*

5

All entities are born, grow, plateau, decline, and die. This progression includes people, animals, and plants. **It applies equally to organizations, civilizations, and empires. They are born, grow, plateau, decline, and die.**

Historians, philosophers, and sociologists have discussed this topic over an extended period of time, including Spengler, Toynbee, Sorkin, and Nisbet.

Reliance on enabling industries

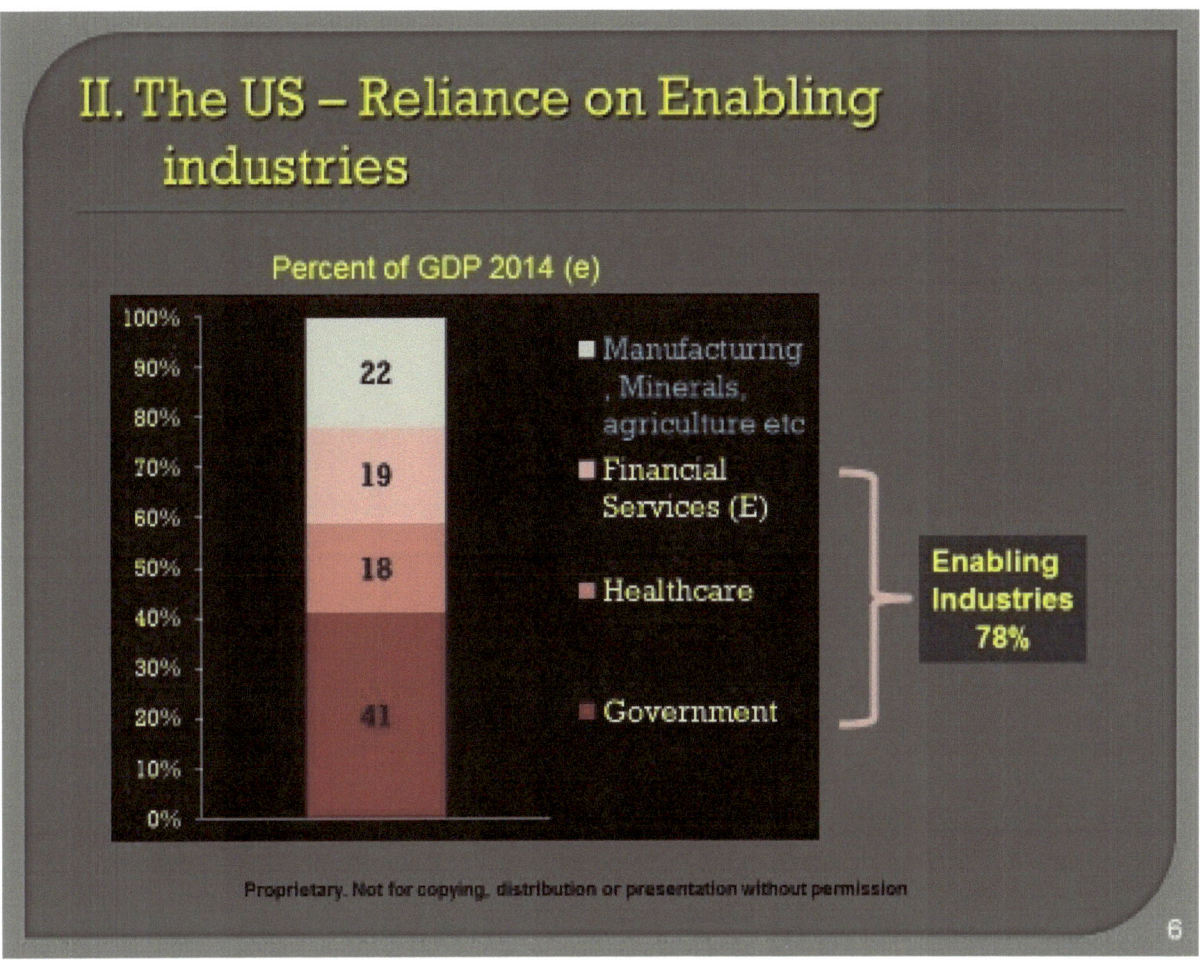

Now let us focus on the U.S. One indicator of the decline of the U.S. is its heavy reliance on enabling industries*, which in 2014 accounted for 78% of the GDP. Non-enabling industries such as manufacturing, minerals, agriculture, and others accounted for 22% of the GDP. The contribution of enabling industries to the GDP in 2014 was a lot higher than it was in the 1950s and 1960s. This will be discussed later in this chapter.

*An enabling industry is one which enables people or other industries to become productive. Examples of enabling industries are the government, healthcare, and financial services. The government provides structure for individuals and companies to work, the healthcare industry provides services so that individuals are healthy and productive, and the financial services industry provides money to people and organizations so they can build and grow.

Government contribution to GDP

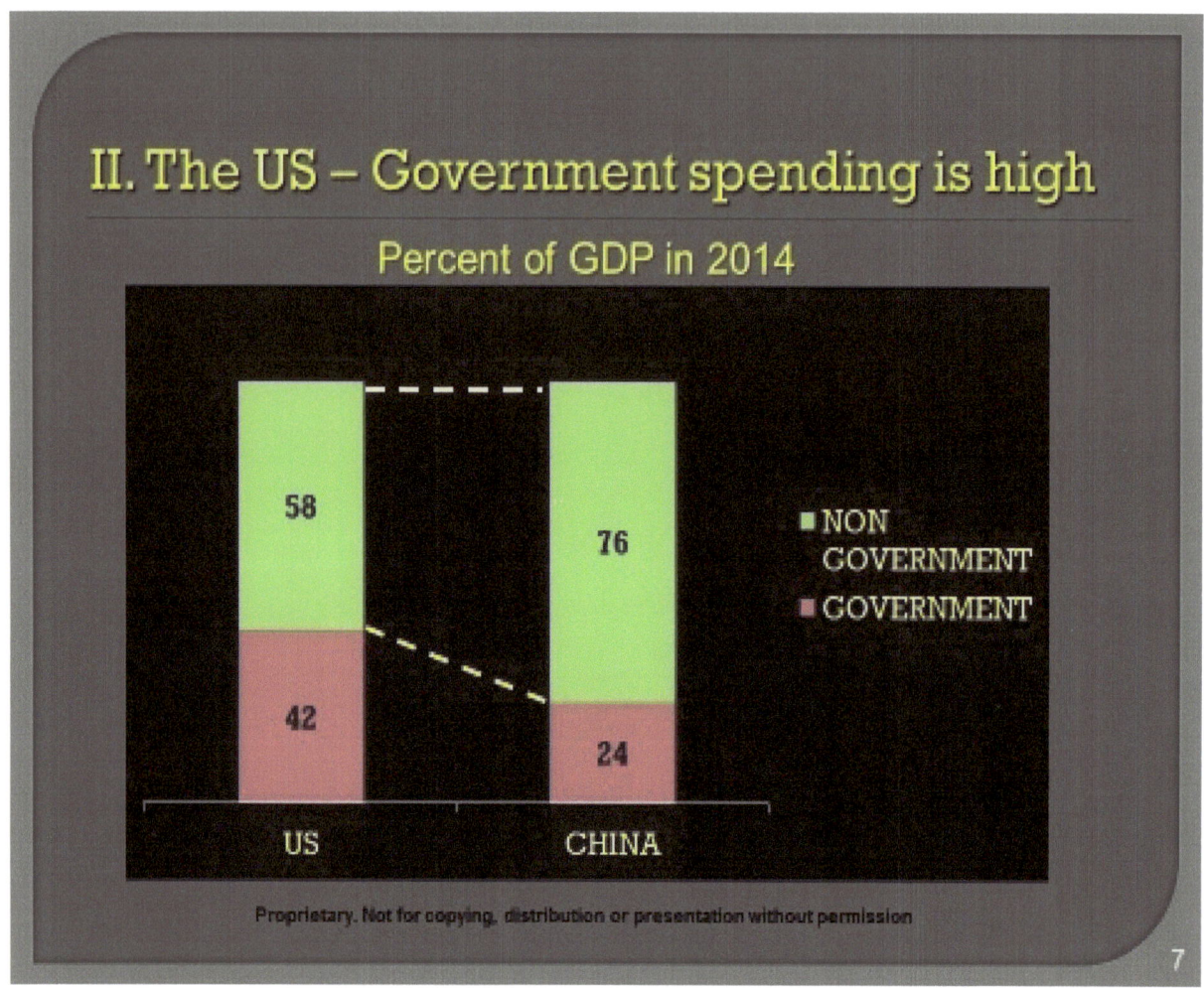

U.S. Government spending is high.

We all know that China is politically a communist country. However, economically, China is more capitalistic than the U.S.

This chart shows that the U.S. Gross Domestic Product (GDP) is divided between the government and the private sector.

In 2014, the federal, state, and local governments accounted for 42% of the U.S. GDP. The private sector accounted for 58% of the GDP.

By contrast, government entities in China account for only 24% of its GDP. The private sector accounts for 76% of GDP. This makes China more economically capitalistic than the U.S.

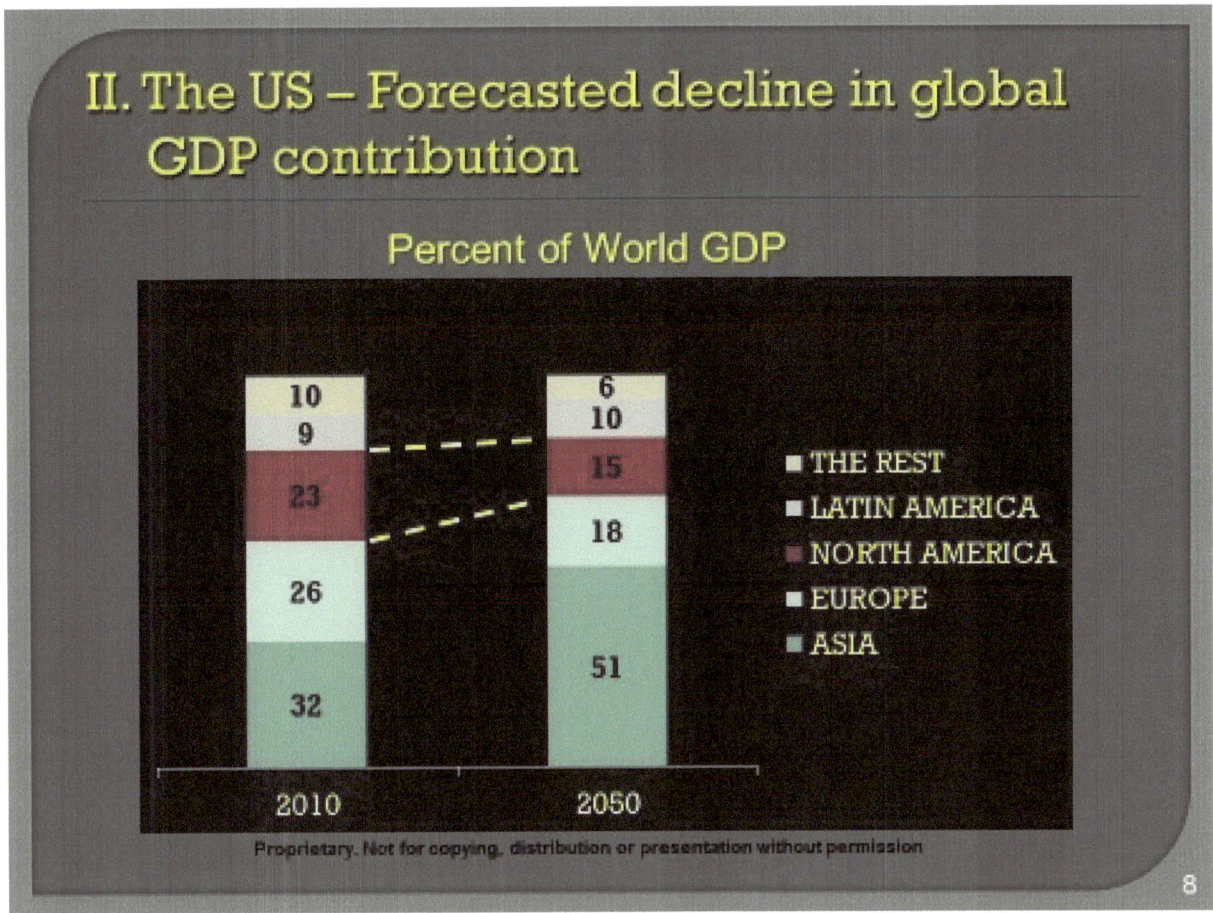

The U.S.'s contribution to the global GDP is forecasted to decline.

In 2010, North America (primarily the U.S. and Canada) accounted for 23% of the world's GDP. That figure is projected to decline to 15% by 2050. Europe is projected to suffer the same fate. It accounted for 26% of the GDP of the world in 2010, forecasted to decline to 18% by 2050. Growth is forecasted to occur in Asia (i.e., China, India, Japan, Korea, Vietnam, Indonesia, and others). Asian countries accounted for 32% of the world's GDP in 2010. By 2050, that figure is projected to grow to 51%. Over the last 5000 years of mankind's history, Asia was the center of economic activity, more often than Europe and the Americas.

This cycle is repeating itself. Asia is once again forecasted to be the center of economic activity and power in the next few decades.

Fiscal and economic decline

II. The US – Areas of decline – Fiscal and Economic

ITEM	CHANGE	PERIOD
Debt (% of GDP)	58% to 102%	25 years
Healthcare Costs (% GDP)	13% to 17%	20 years
Enabling Industries (% GDP)	61% to 78%	20 years
Contribution to world GDP (%)	23% to 25%	30 years
Projected decline in contribution (2010 to 2050)	35%	40 years
Fragile state index (Score)	34.5 to 35.3	9 years

9

The U.S. has experienced fiscal and economic decline in several areas. Over a period of 25 years, U.S. debt increased from 58% of the GDP to 102%.

The country's healthcare contribution to GDP increased from 13% to over 17% in twenty years, increasing the costs of products manufactured in the U.S.

Enabling industries' contribution increased from 61% to 78% of the GDP in twenty years at the expense of other segments of the economy e.g. manufacturing.

The only stable element has been the U.S.'s past contribution to the global GDP, which has remained at around 23 to 25%.

However, the contribution of the U.S. and Canada to the world GDP is projected to decline by 35 percentage points (from 23% to 15%) by 2050.

The final measure demonstrating the decline of the U.S. is the Fragile States Index*. The U.S. score went up from 34.5 to 35.3 in nine years, which means the U.S. has become less stable.

*Fragile States Index is a score that identifies how stable a country is based on a number of political, economic, financial, and demographic criteria. The higher the score, the lower the stability.

II. The US – Areas of decline – Scientific and literature

ITEM	CHANGE	PERIOD
High School Science rank	9 to 27	22 years
High School Math ranking	12 to 35	22 years
Share of Nobel Prizes (%)	73% to 54%	21 years
Number of US origin patents (variance from mean)	21% above to 4% below	21 years

10

The next area of U.S. decline is found in science and literature. The U.S. declined in many rankings, including the following:

- From 9th to 27th in high school science rankings in 22 years
- From 12th to 35th in high school math rankings in 22 years
- From 73% to 54% in share of Nobel Prizes in 21 years
- Twenty-one years ago, patents that were generated in the U.S. were 21% above average of all patents worldwide. Today that figure is 4% lower than the worldwide average.

II. The US – Areas of decline – Social and Political

ITEM	CHANGE	PERIOD
Corruption ranking	14 to 16	15 years
Press Freedom ranking	32 to 49	2 years
Ease of doing business ranking	3 to 7	6 years
Life expectancy ranking	51 to 53	5 years

11

The next area of U.S. decline is social and political. The U.S. has declined in the following areas:

- From 14th to 16th in the global corruption ranking in 15 years
- From 32nd to 49th in press freedom ranking in two years – a precipitous drop
- From 3rd to 7th in ease of doing business ranking in six years
- From 51st to 53rd in life expectancy ranking in five years.

Relative to other empires

II. The US – Relative to other Empires

Empire/Civilization	Approximate Period	Length (Years)	% of world population at peak
Greek (Macedonian)	808 – 179 BC	629	40 (est.)
Persian*	658 BC – 651 AD	1309	35
Roman	27 BC – 1453 AD	1480	38
Islamic/Ottoman	632 – 1923	1291	23
Mongol	1206 – 1370	164	26
Spanish	1436 – 1808	372	12
Ming Dynasty	1368 - 1644	276	29
Qing Dynasty	1644 – 1912	268	37
Russian	1721 – 1917	196	10
British	1583 – 1997	414	20
USA	**1776 – 2015 +**	**237 +**	**5**

12

This table shows a comparison of the U.S. to the other empires that we discussed previously. The U.S. started as a country in 1776; this means that the U.S. has been a country and a civilization for 237 years up to this point. How much longer will it last?

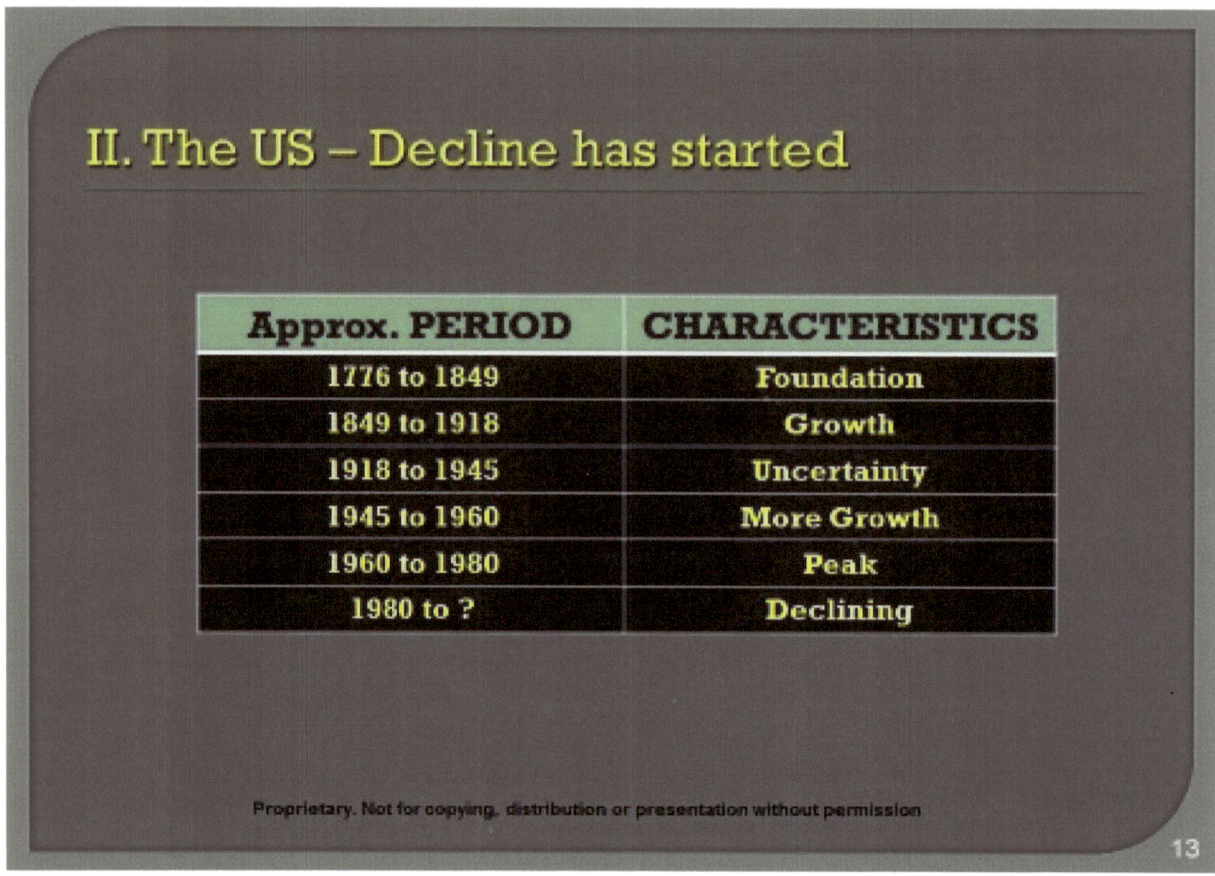

The decline of the U.S. has already begun, as is evident in the following approximate time periods:

1776 to 1849 was a period of foundation.

1849 to 1918 was a period of growth.

1918 to 1945 was a period of uncertainty with the two world wars.

From 1945 to 1960, the U.S. saw more growth, because most of Europe was devastated after the Second World War.

During the period of 1960 to 1980 the U.S. peaked.

At around 1980, the U.S. began its decline.

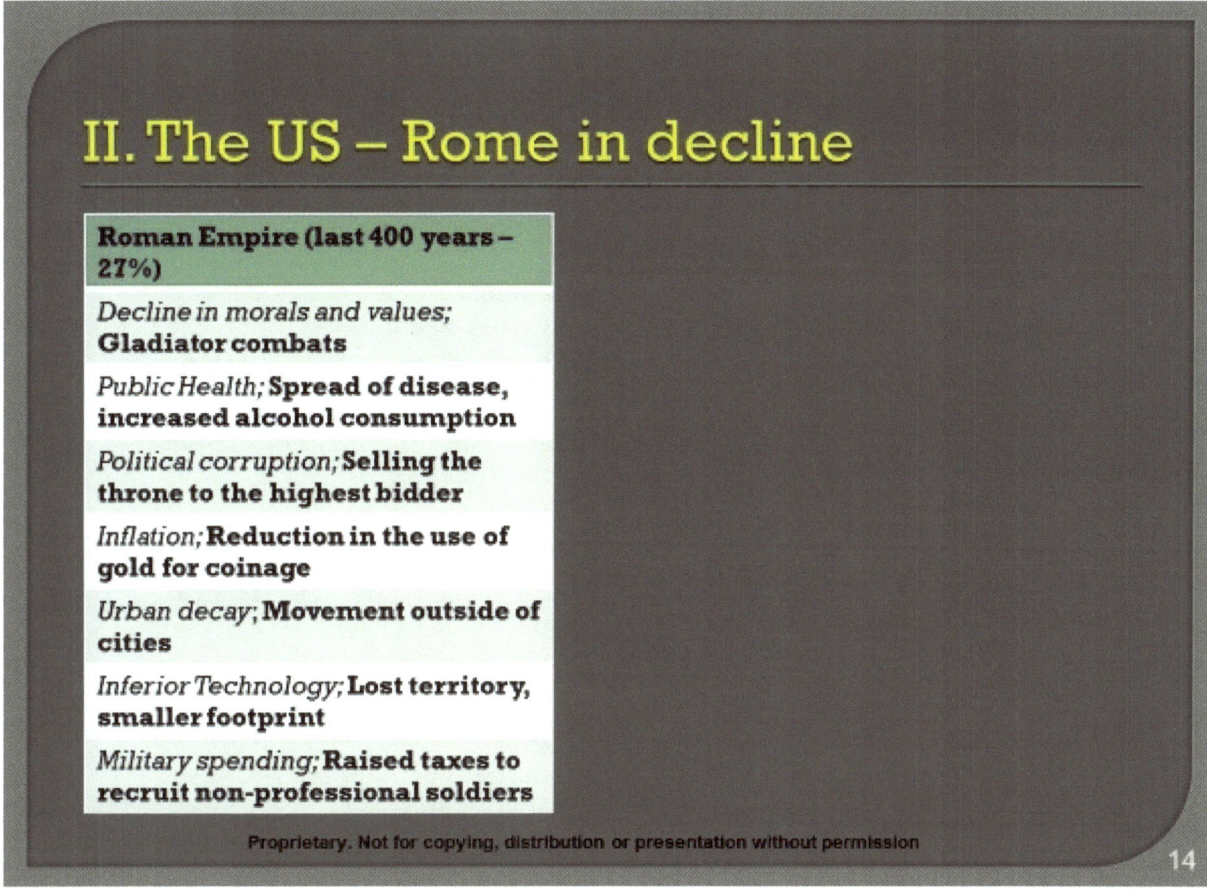

Examination of Rome during its period of decline (the last 400 years of a 1,500-year era) reveals some of the indicators of decline, as follows:

Morals and values – Gladiator combat

Public health – Increase in the spread of disease and alcohol consumption

Political corruption – Selling of the throne (literally) to the highest bidder

Inflation – Reduction in the use of gold for coinage because people were using gold for jewelry and other purposes, leading to increased inflation

Urban decay – Increased movement outside the cities

Inferior technology – Loss of territory because technology became inferior when other countries and civilizations began to encroach upon it

Military spending – Taxes were raised to recruit nonprofessional mercenary soldiers as opposed to citizen soldiers

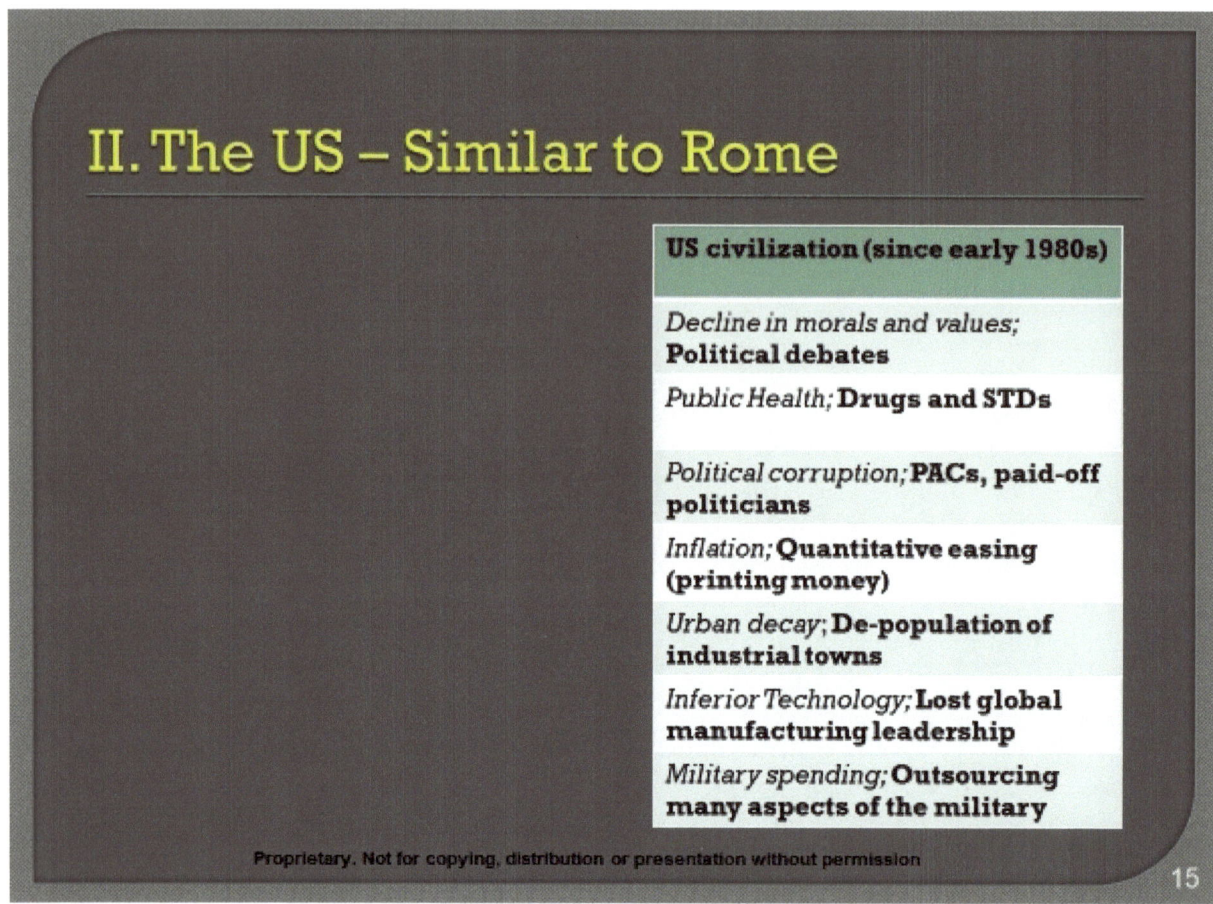

Now we move forward 2,000 years to the establishment of the U.S., and while some of these aspects are not directly applicable, there are many likenesses:

Morals and values – Political debates look like gladiator combat

Public health – Increase in STDs and drug use

Political corruption – Politicians being paid off, and influenced by, special interests

Inflation - Quantitative easing (printing money without collateral)

Urban decay - The depopulation of industrial towns

Inferior technology - Lost global manufacturing leadership and increase in the contribution of enabling industries (discussed previously)

Military spending - Outsourcing many aspects of the military to the private sector whose primary motivation is income

Reasons for the U.S. decline

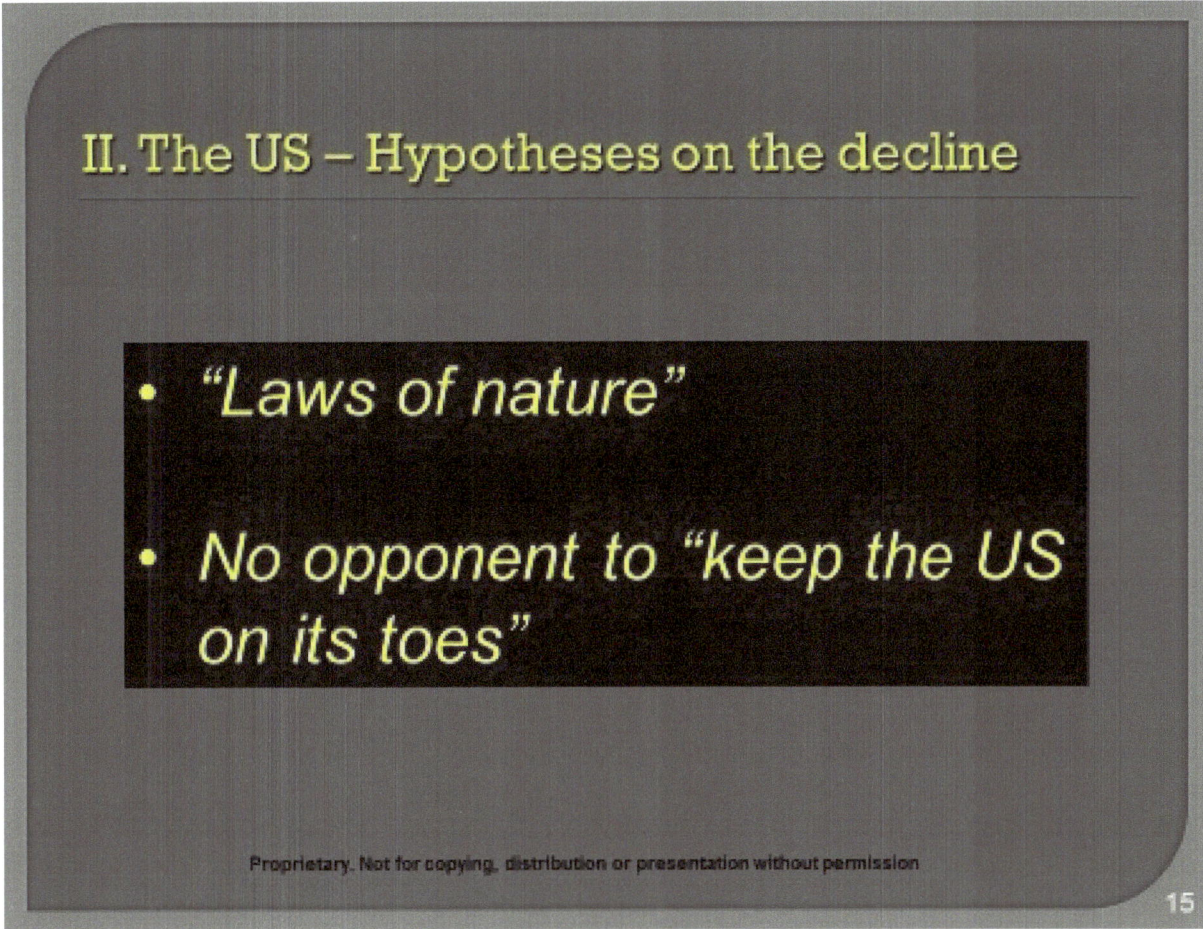

Why is the U.S. declining? I have a couple of possible hypotheses:

Firstly, the laws of nature dictate that, just like every empire and civilization before, the U.S. was born, it grows, it peaks, it plateaus, and it declines.

The second one is a more interesting hypothesis:

The U.S. is very good at competition, which is why it excels in sports. We thrive when we have an opponent to compete with; it keeps U.S. on our toes. In the early eighties, the Soviet Union collapsed. We then no longer had a global opponent to compete with on ideas and philosophy. We began to decline because there was no opponent to motivate U.S. to be the best.

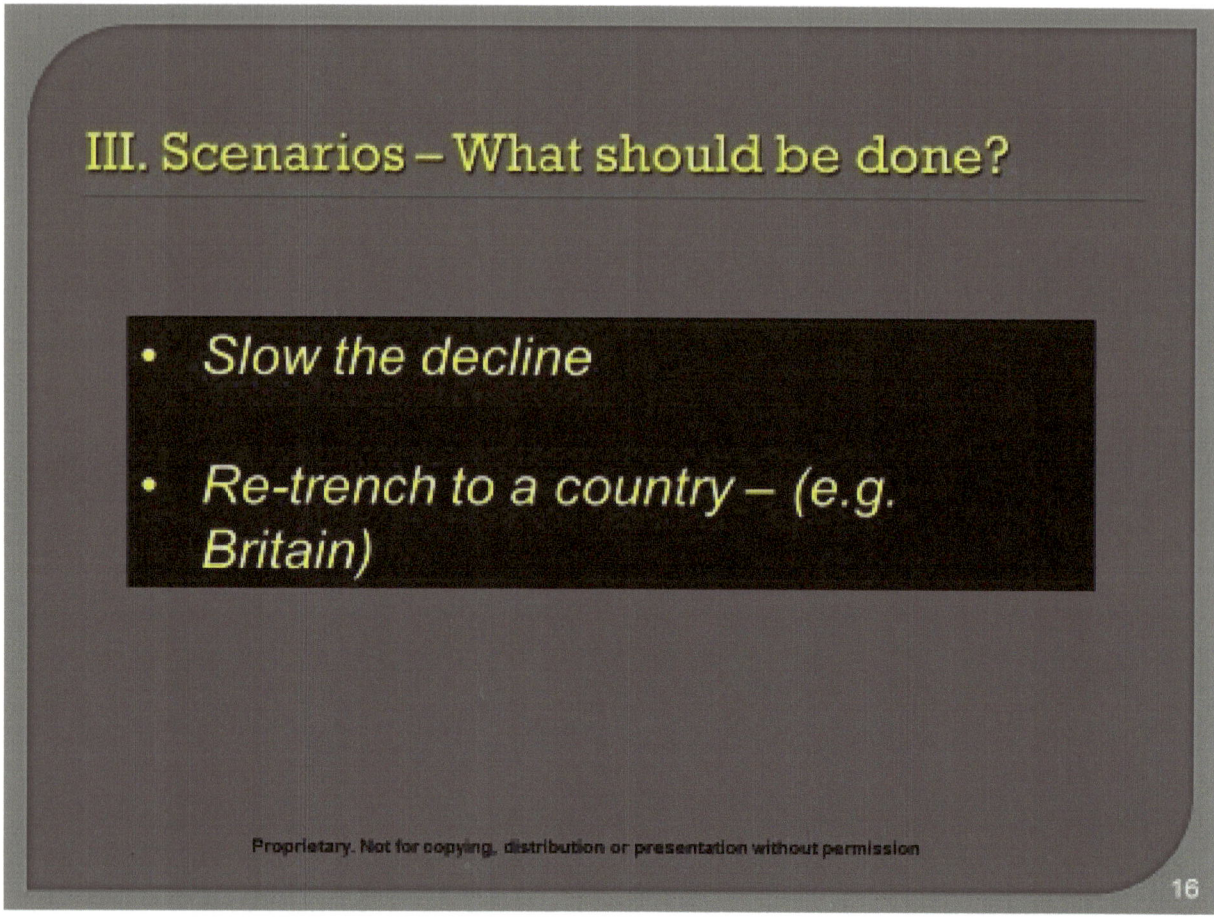

Now we'll talk about scenarios for re-positioning the U.S.

There are two possible scenarios to preserve the U.S. as a global superpower: The first is to slow down the decline, but to keep the U.S. as the worldwide leading superpower and civilization. The second is to retrench to a country, just like Britain did when it lost its empire. It re-trenched back to a democratic Island nation with an "affiliation" with its former colonies. In management terms, this is called "sticking to the knitting" – in other words, leveraging your core strengths and not relying on your weaknesses.

In either of these cases, for the U.S. to leverage its strengths, it needs to go back to the original concept of its creation, a country composed of 50 states under a federal umbrella. This concept is what made it competitive and growth driven (this will be discussed in more detail in the next chapter). It is no wonder that the Founding Fathers named this country "The United States of America", not the "The Republic of America."

Repositioning the United States.

This presentation discusses the possible solutions for repositioning the United States, utilizing good old-fashioned management practices. It is contrary to the historical practice of centralizing more decisions at the federal level.

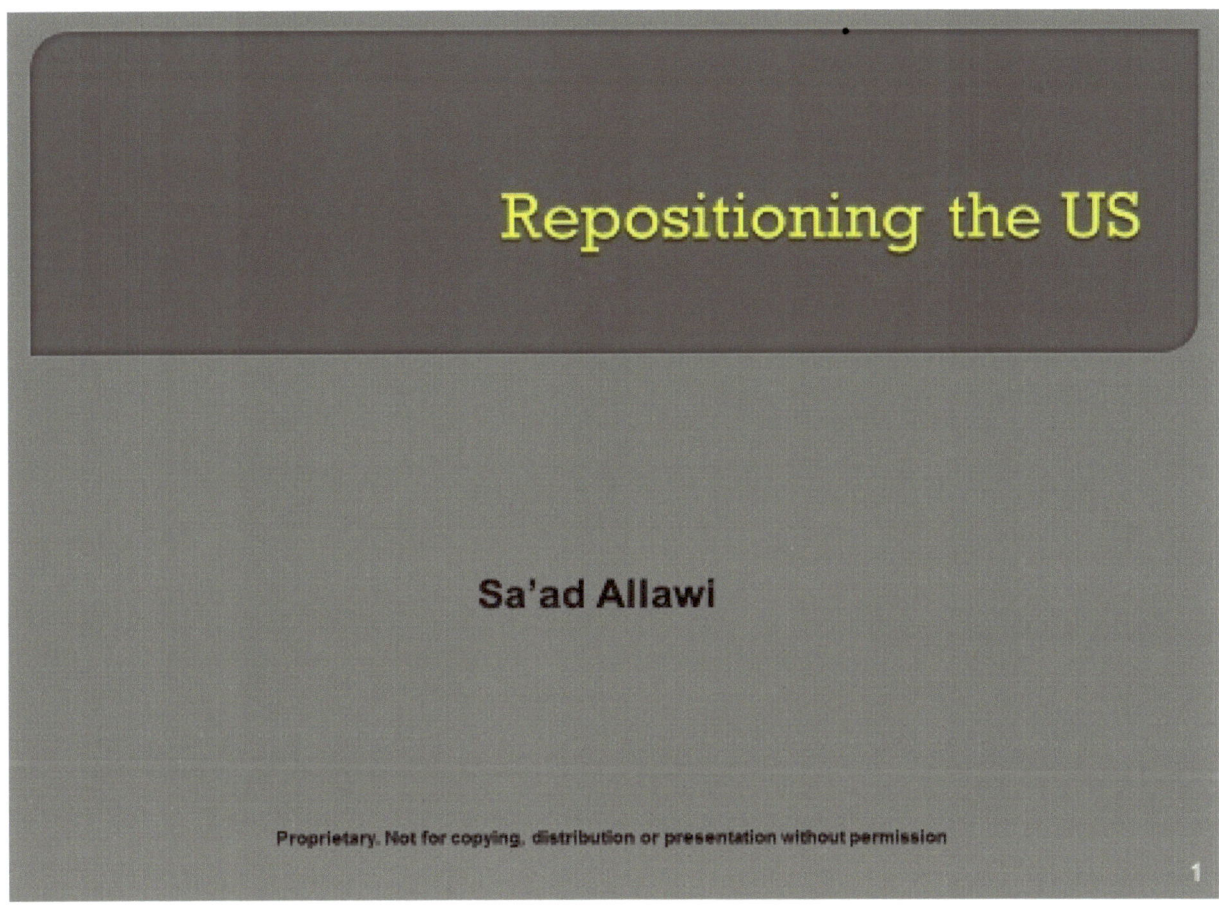

This presentation discusses the possible ways to reposition the U.S. for the two scenarios discussed in Chapter IV. It utilizes McKinsey's 7-S framework from the best seller, <u>In Search of Excellence</u>, to develop sound management practices at the national level and suggests actions at the individual level.

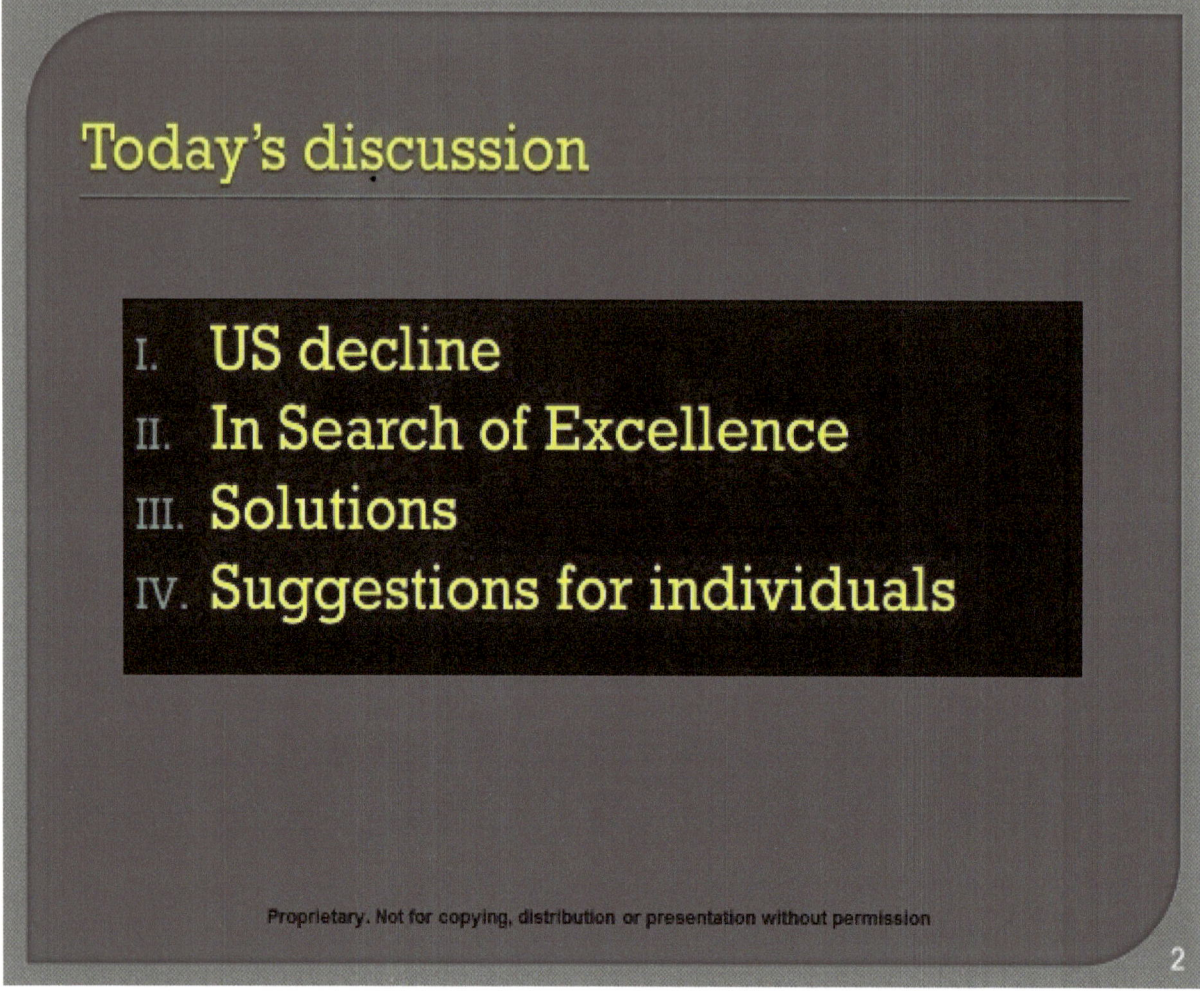

This presentation covers four items: a recap from the prior presentation on the decline of the U.S., an overview of a proven template for successful change as discussed in the book <u>In Search of Excellence</u>, solutions based on best management practices, and suggestions at the personal level.

I. US decline – Recap

- Increasing reliance on enabling industries
- Heavier reliance on government, compared to other growth economies
- Declining share of global GDP
- Decline in Fiscal and Economic measures
- Decline in Scientific and Literature measures
- Decline in Social and Political measures

Proprietary. Not for copying, distribution or presentation without permission

3

In review of the decline of the U.S., the U.S. has demonstrated increasing reliance on enabling industries, heavier reliance on the government compared to other growth economies such as China's, a projected decline in the share of global GDP over the next forty years, a decline in fiscal and economic measures, a decline in scientific and literature measures, and a decline in social and political measures.

Two scenarios

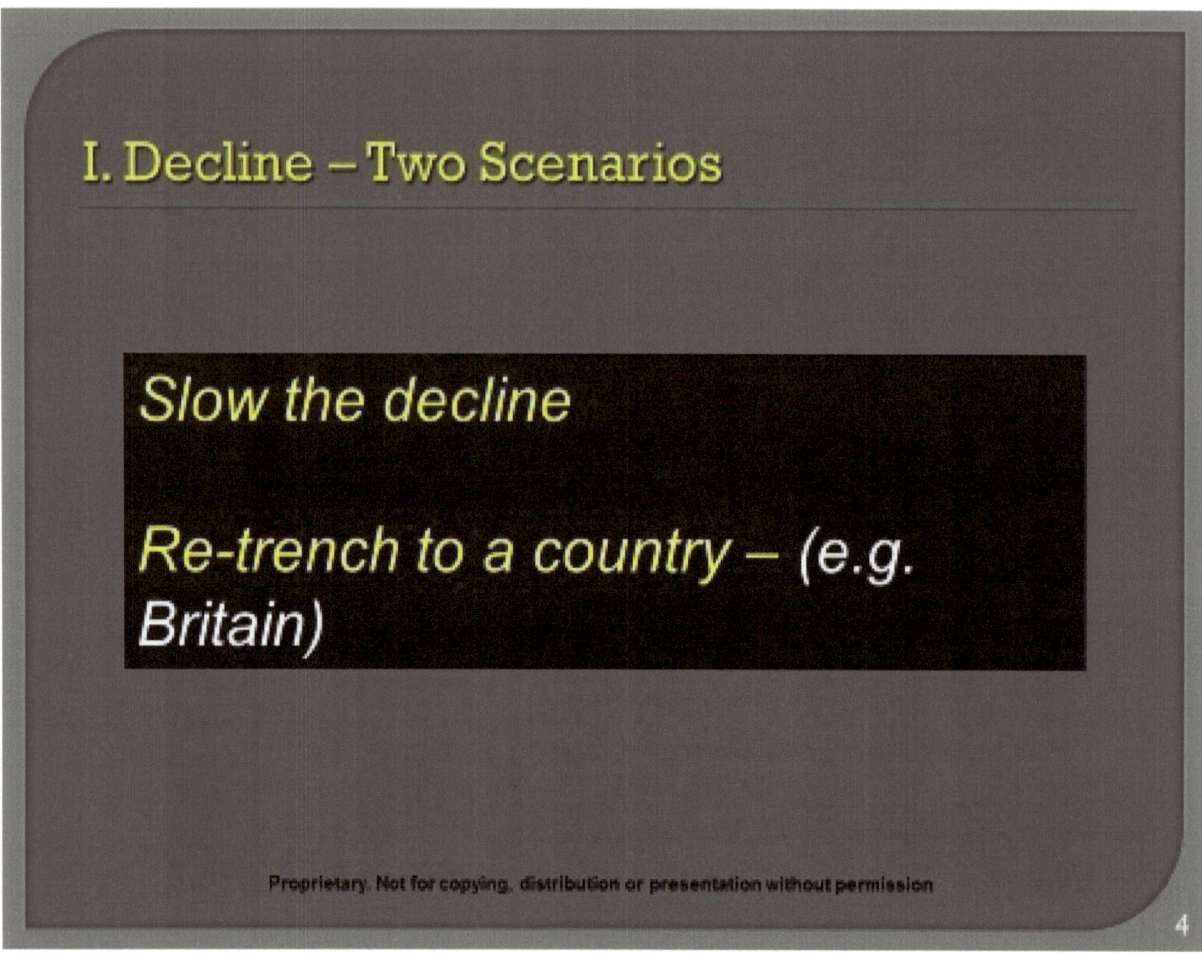

I. Decline – Two Scenarios

Slow the decline

Re-trench to a country – (e.g. Britain)

4

Two scenarios were mentioned in the previous presentation: the first involves the U.S. continuing as a major superpower and preeminent civilization while slowing the decline, and in the second, the U.S. retrenches to a country, just as Britain did after it lost its empire.

Template – In Search of Excellence

For the purposes of this presentation, the template that will be used is one that has been used for years by practitioners of large-scale organizational change. It is discussed in the book called <u>In Search of Excellence</u>, published in the early 1980s by two McKinsey partners, Tom Peters and Bob Waterman. This work incorporates lessons from America's best-run companies, many of whom are multi-national corporations. The book was a best seller for many years. Its enduring template is still in use today – including by the author himself.

Seven "S"s

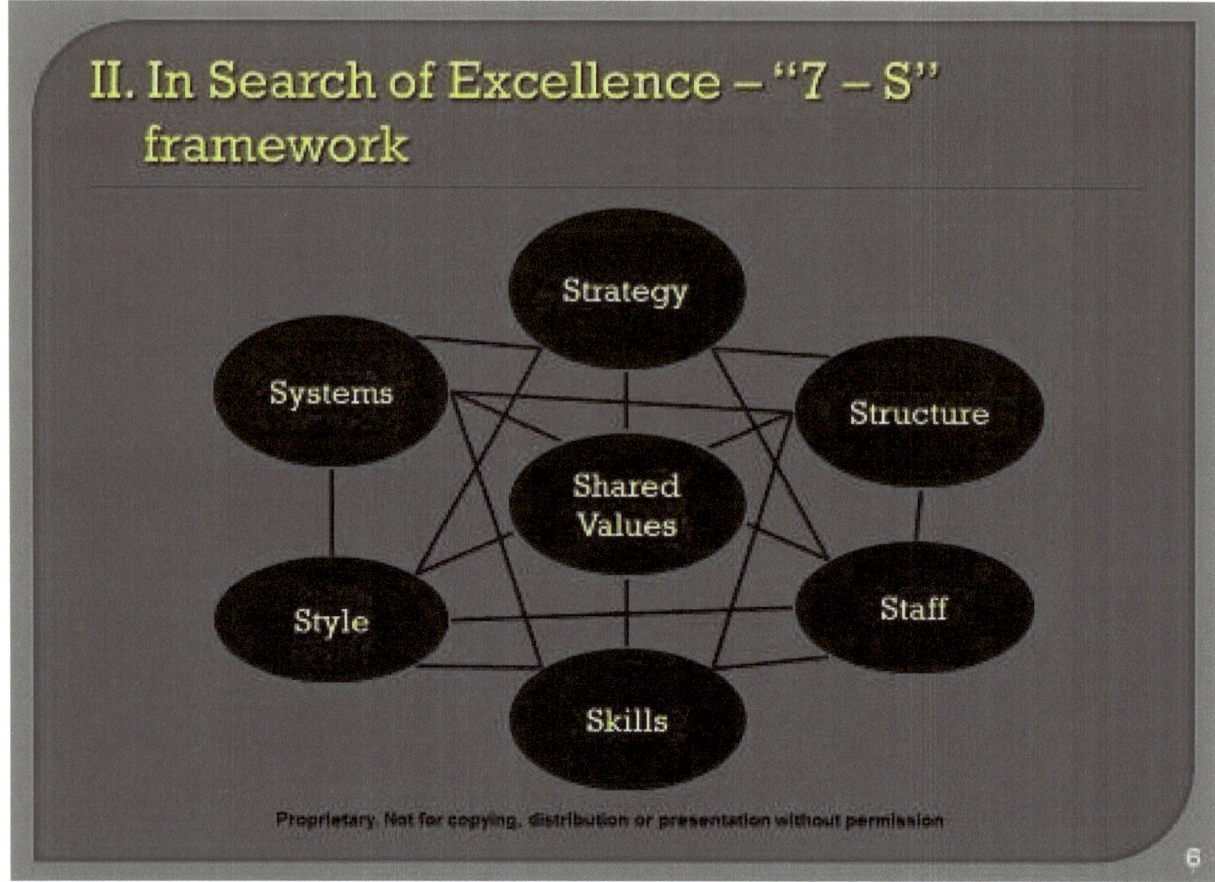

The template that we will be using, has seven S's.

Starting in the middle is **Shared Values**, which refers to the mission; i.e., what is the mission of the organization?

At the twelve o'clock position is **Strategy**; i.e., how do you make your mission a reality?

Moving clockwise we have **Structure**, which refers to the reporting relationships between people in an organization (lines and boxes) and accountability.

Next, **Staff**: How many people do you need to run the organization, of what type, and where are they located?

Skills: What are the core competencies required to run the organization?

Style: What management style is used; e.g. a top-down or bottom-up approach, or competitive or collaborative?

And finally, **Systems**: This involves management, procedures, and practices as well as information technology systems.

Approach

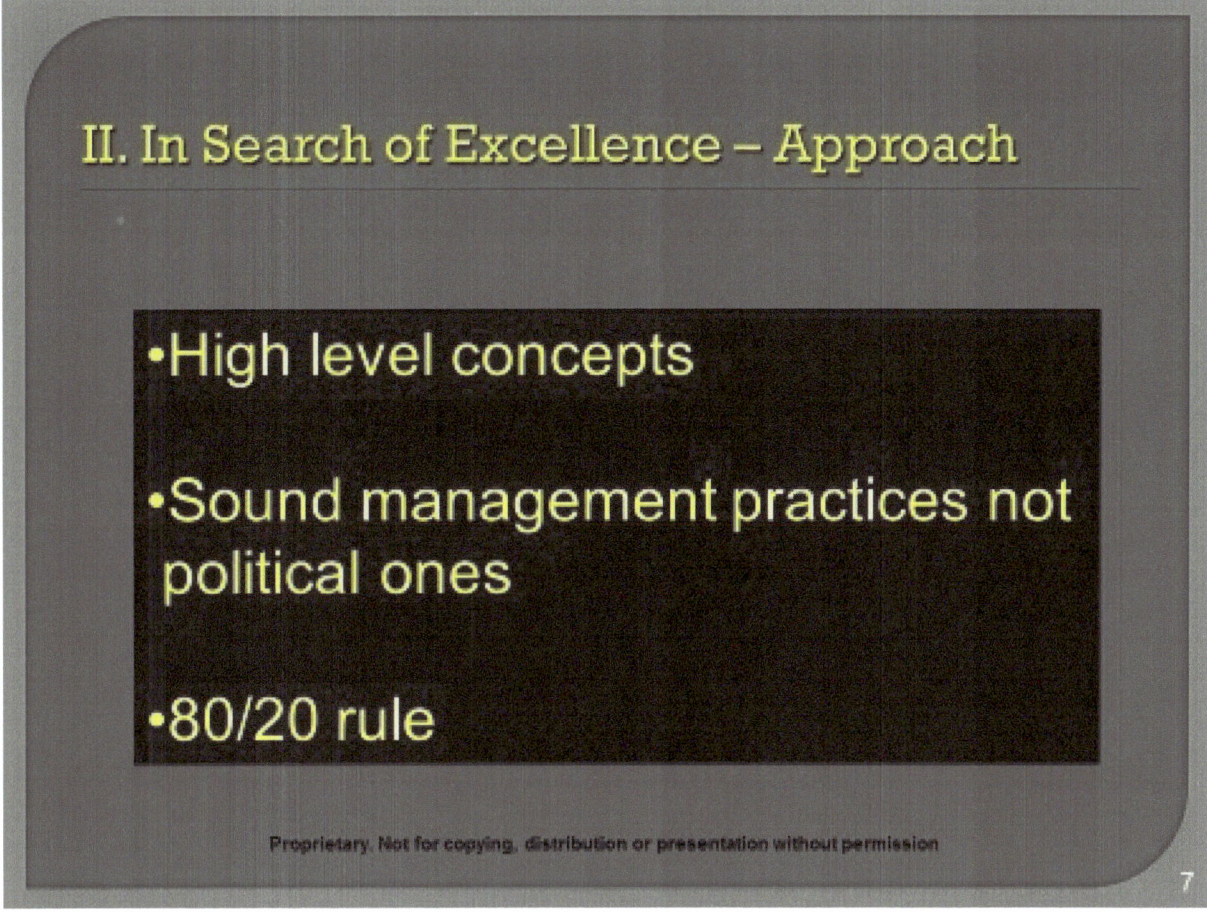

The approach utilized in this presentation is as follows: Recommendations are high-level concepts and are not detailed tactical solutions. They are based on sound management practices, not political ones, and they are based on the 80-20 rule. In other words, what is the fewest number of "levers" you need to pull to give you 80% of the benefits?

Let's start with shared values (mission). Traditionally, people in the United States felt optimistic about current and future opportunities. That optimism has all but disappeared. In 2003, 58 percent of the people in this country expressed the feeling that the country is heading in the wrong direction. **This number is now over 75 percent**

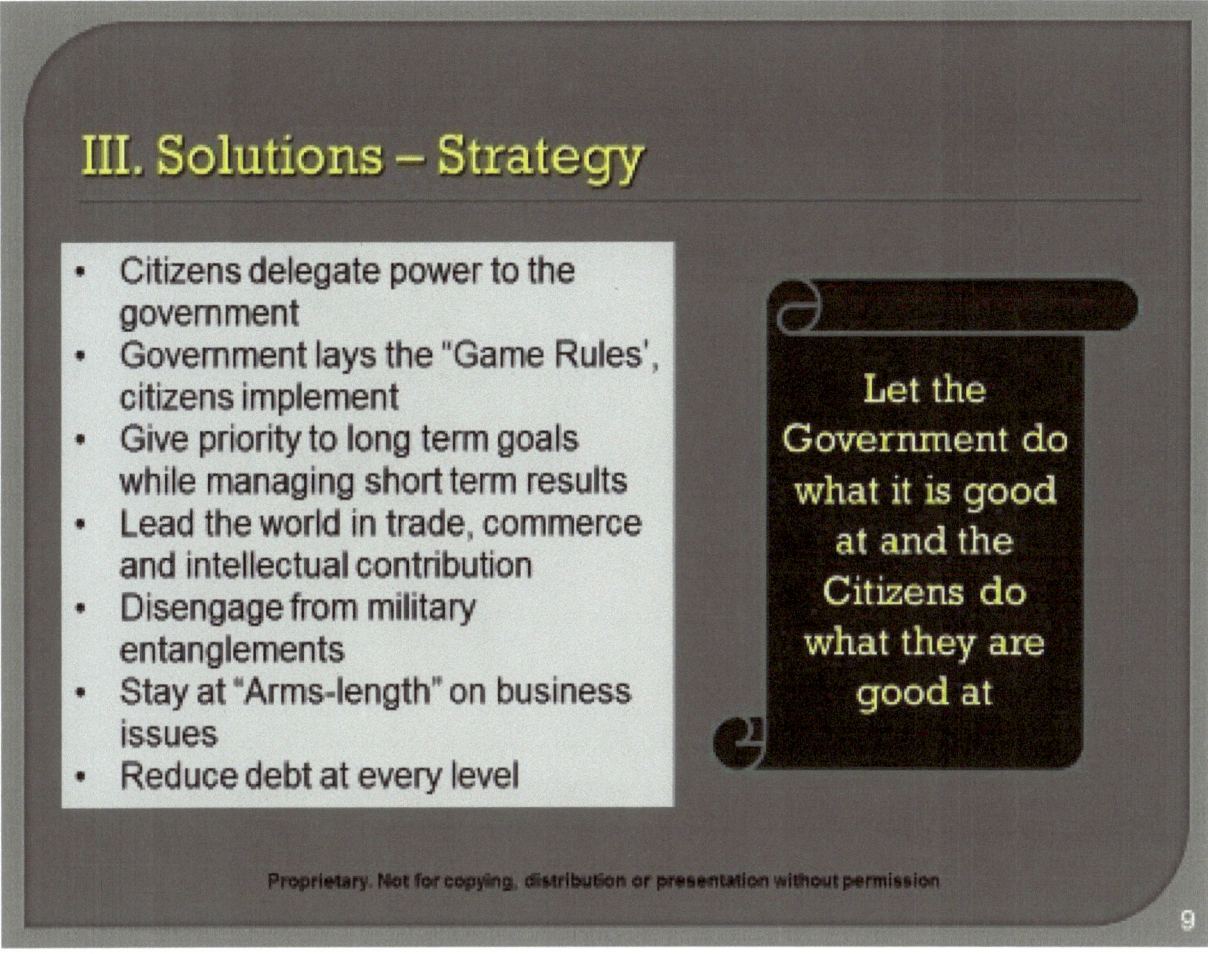

In terms of strategy, some of the best practices in the past have been as follows:

- Citizens delegate power to the government
- The government lays the game rules and the citizens implement them
- Priorities are given to long-term goals while managing short-term results
- The U.S. leads the world in trade, commerce, and intellectual contribution
- Unnecessary military entanglements are avoided
- The U.S. stays at arm's length from business issues
- Leaders strive to reduce debt at every level

In other words, the government should do what it is good at, and the citizens should do what they are good at.

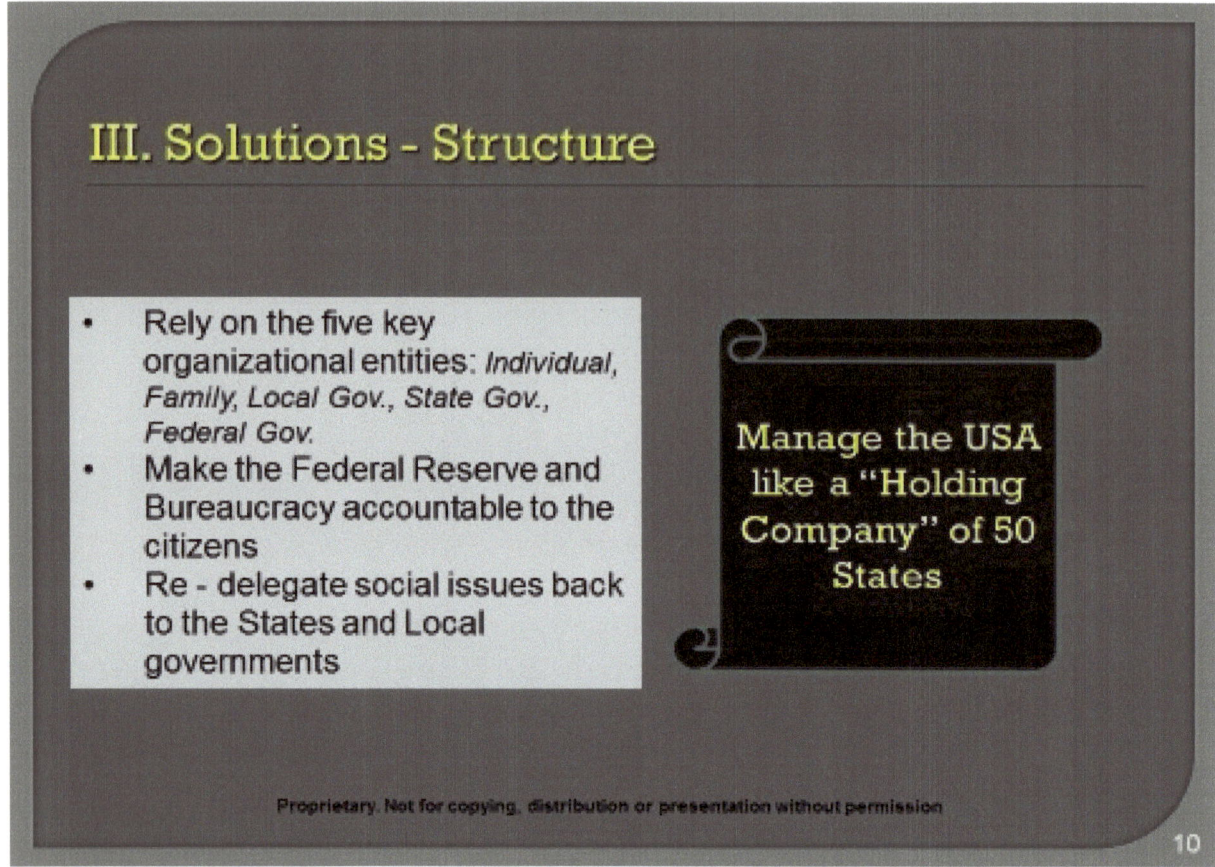

Best practices related to structure (accountability and reporting relationships) involve, first, reliance on five key organizational entities: individual, family, local government, state government, and federal government, in that order. Second, the federal reserve and bureaucracy should be made accountable to the citizens. These two major federal agencies are not currently directly accountable to the citizens. Third, social practices (e.g. Health, Education, Marriage) must be re-delegated back to the state and local governments. This one is very important; if the federal government maintains control over social practices, one of two things are likely to happen: (1) A majority supported practice will require imposing the will of that majority on the minority and take away the minority's right or (2) A minority supported practice will be imposed on the will of the majority. Neither of these practices will work, and neither of them are constitutional. Large corporate entities have discovered that, if they want to grow, they decentralize activities and decisions to the division or business units with a high degree of autonomy (holding company model). General Electric Company is a good example of a strong growth, highly decentralized organization.

In order to slow the decline and grow again, the U.S. will need to be managed like a holding company by decentralizing activities back to the States and providing a high degree of autonomy.

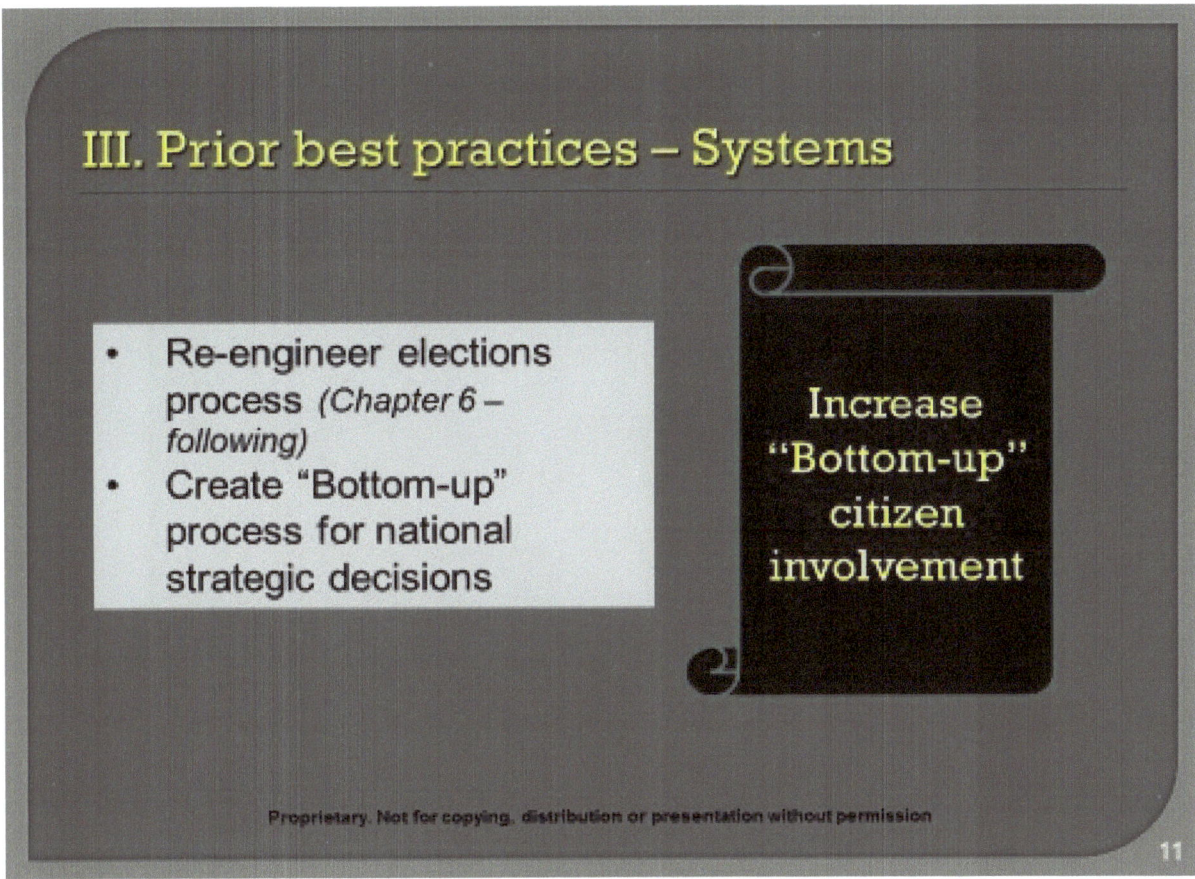

The best practices for systems include reengineering the federal elections system (more on this in the next chapter) and offering the citizens a bigger say in the country's strategic direction through a bottom-up process.

In other words, create a way for involving citizens in the direction of the country – Grassroots Metamorphosis

Style

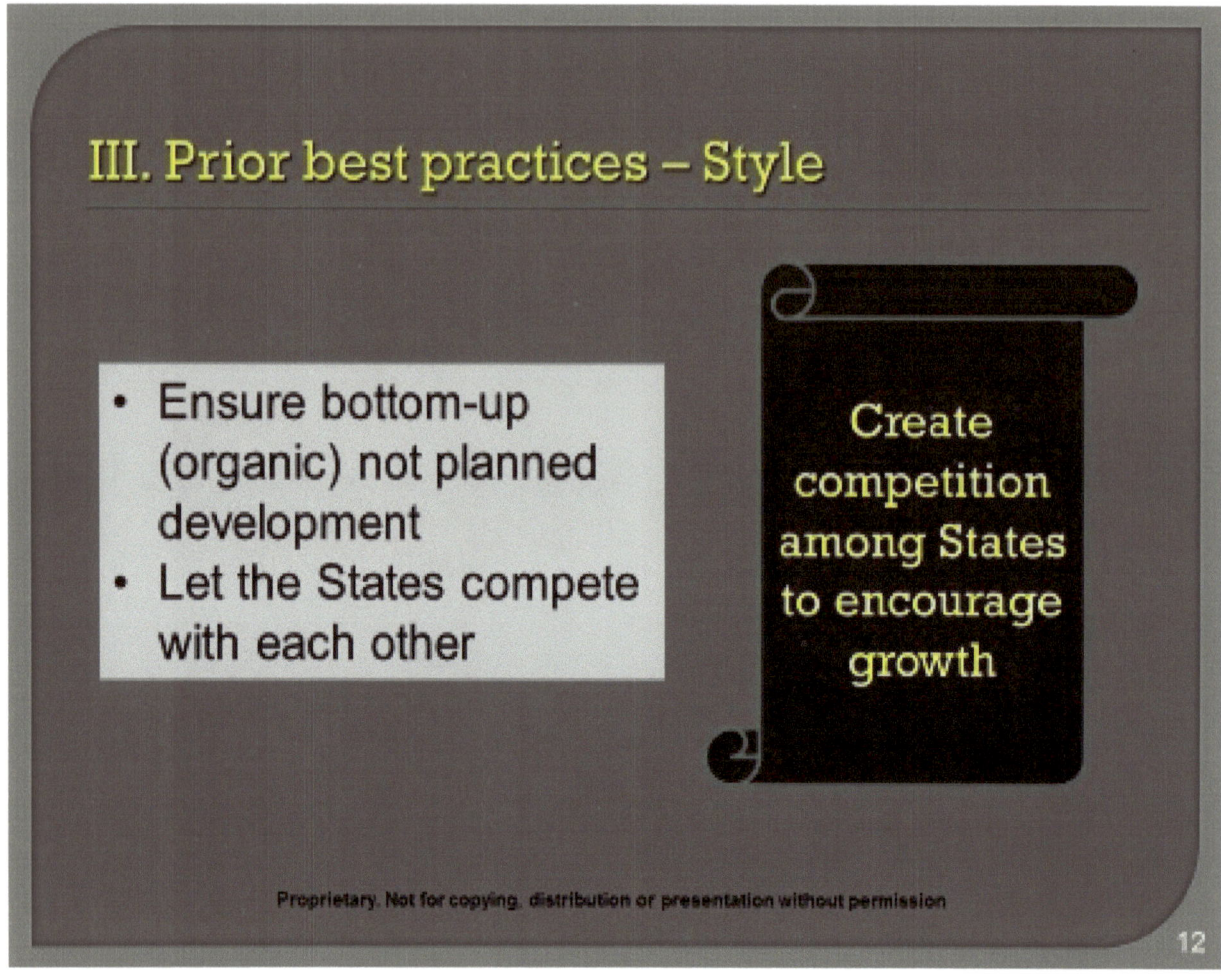

In terms of style, best practices include bottom-up organic (not top-down planned) development. One of the core competencies of the U.S. is the ability of its citizens to take risks and create new opportunities. This is organic bottom-up growth; the U.S. was built on this competency. The country is not particularly effective at developing centralized plans which are then decentralized for people to implement. This is called planned top-down growth. China does this effectively, and the Soviet Union previously practiced this.

The citizens of this country also perform best when they engage in constructive competition. For this country to grow again, we need to unleash that organic bottom-up growth model.

In order to do so, the U.S. needs to create competition among the States, which has been disappearing as of late.

Skills

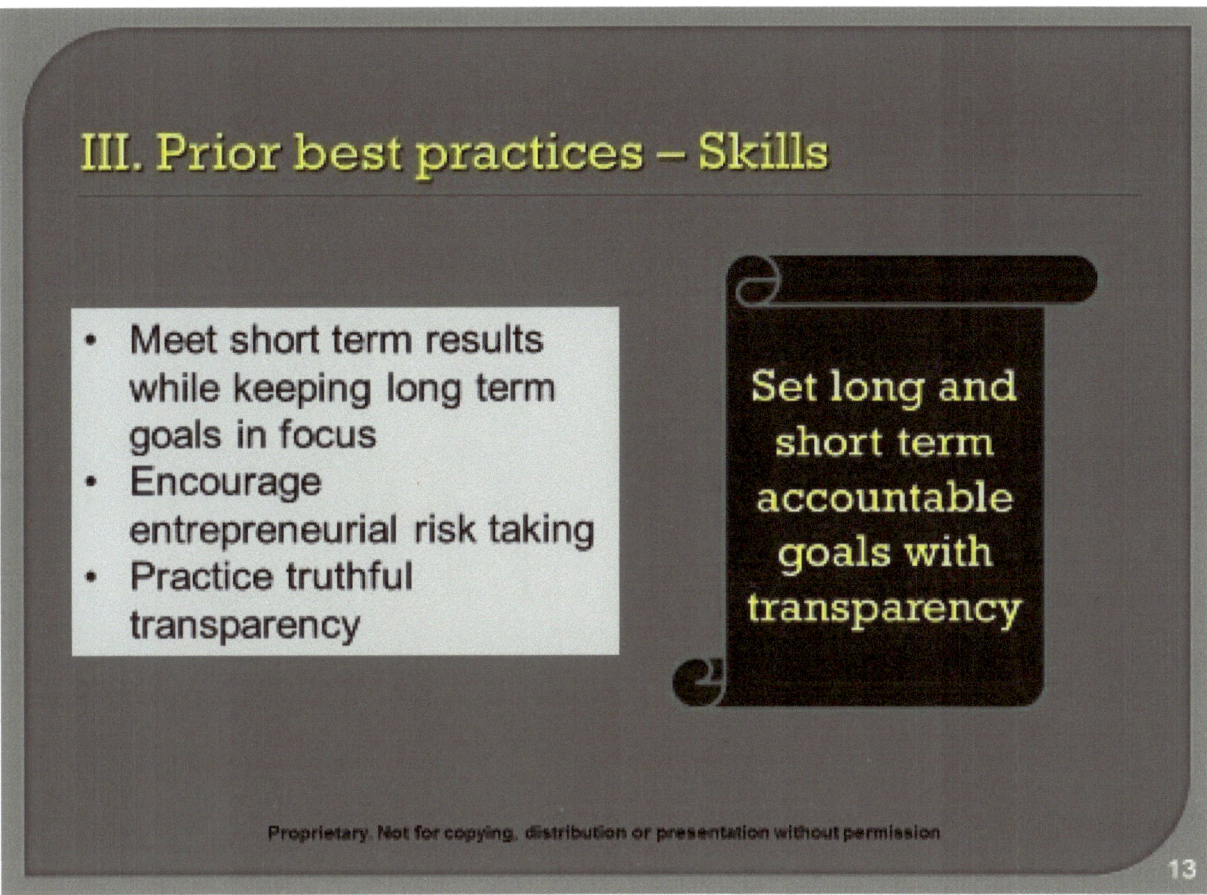

Prior best practices in skills:

We have in the past met short-term results while keeping long-term goals in focus. This country and many of its businesses are now much more oriented toward short-term goals, and they've lost their overall focus. on long-term goals. There is a saying in business: U.S. companies manage for **next quarter results**, whereas companies in Japan (and now China) manage for **next quarter century results**.

To implement these best practices, we must encourage entrepreneurial risk-taking again to revitalize growth and practice truthful transparency.

In essence, we need to deliver long-term results and ensure that the short-term results are consistent with those long-term goals, all in an accountable and transparent manner.

Staff

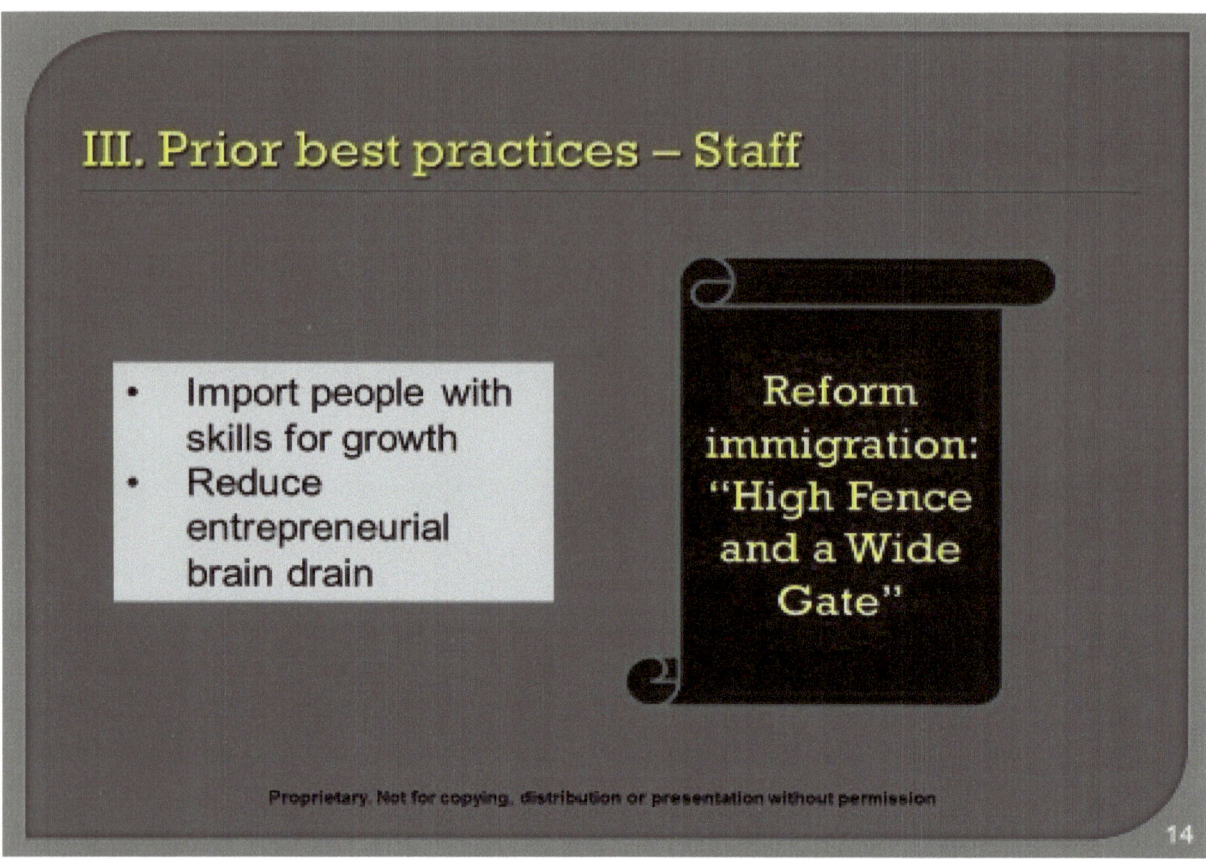

In terms of staff, best practices include importing people with skills for growth and reducing entrepreneurial brain drain if we want to maintain a leadership position in the world in technology and intellectual property.

In essence, what we'd like to do is reform immigration and create a metaphorical "high fence and a wide gate." A "high fence" stops people from coming into the U.S. illegally, while a "wide gate" makes it easy for those who want to contribute to the growth to enter and work in the U.S.

Consistent with the intent

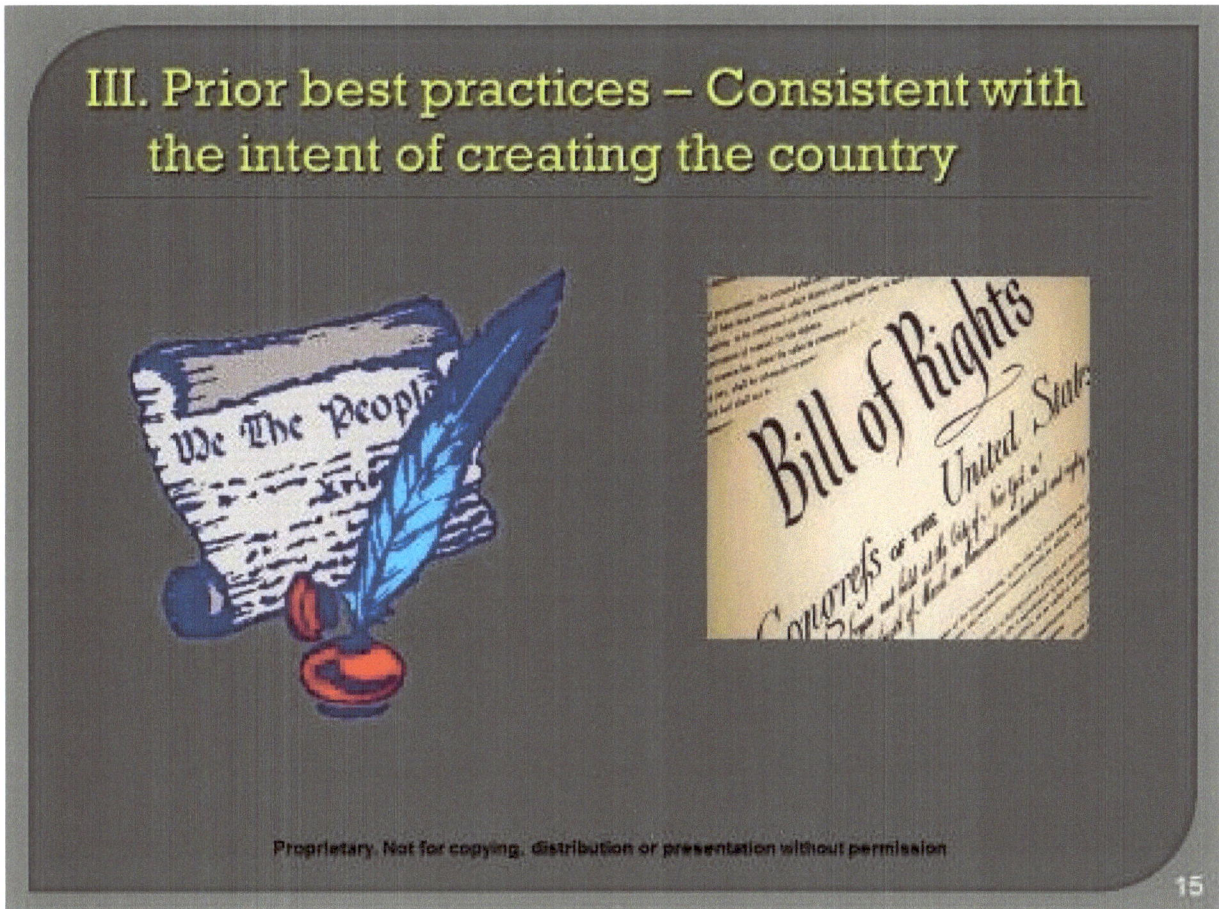

All of the best practices mentioned earlier are consistent with the intent of creating the country—in terms of both the Constitution and the Bill of Rights.

This is not new information. The founding fathers were very pragmatic when they were involved in developing the Bill of Rights and the Constitution. They applied these pragmatic and practical principles during the creation of these documents.

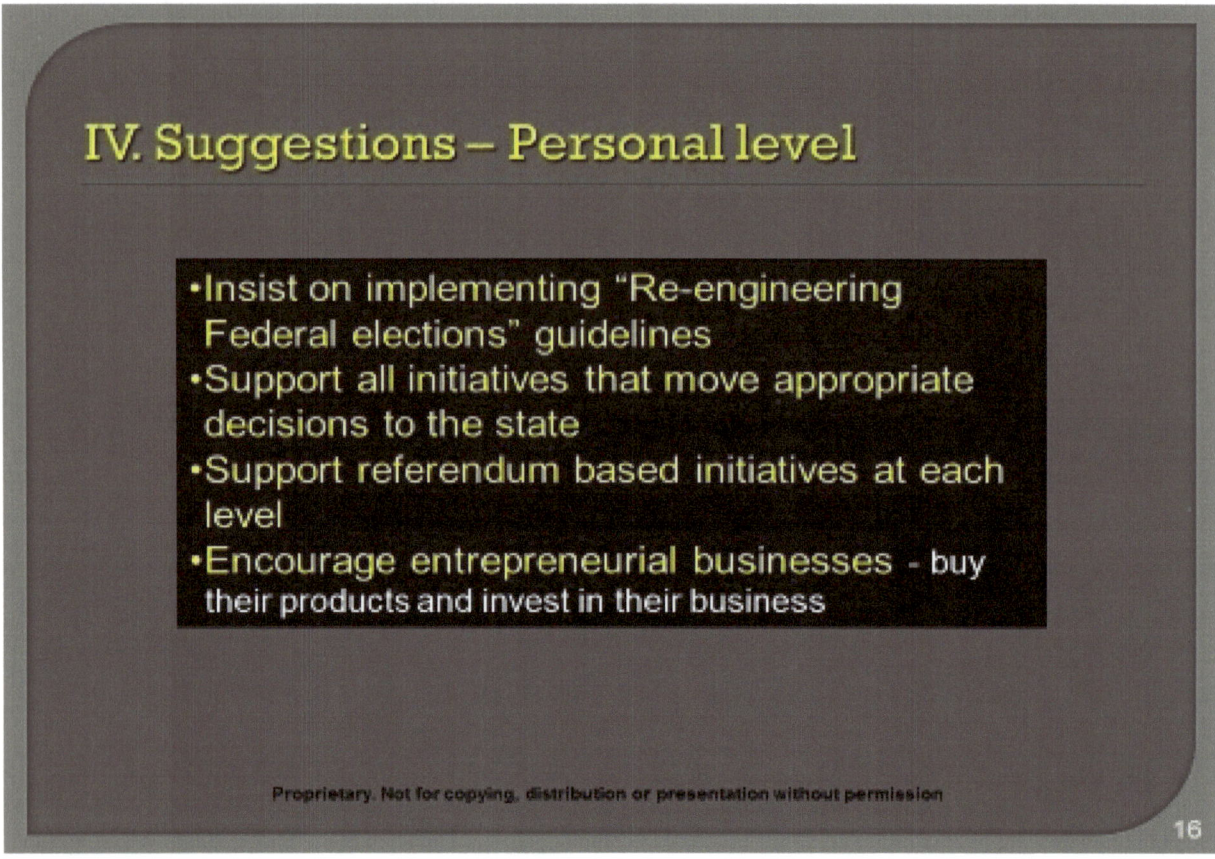

So, what can we do at the personal level?

We can actively participate in implementing reengineering federal election guidelines in the following chapter; support all initiatives that move appropriate decisions on to the state and push back against inappropriate initiatives that look like they're heading in a federal direction; support referendum-based initiatives at each level by pushing your representatives at the local, state, and federal levels to ensure your participation and that of other citizens in strategic decisions; and encourage entrepreneurial businesses, buy their products, and invest in them.

Chapter 2
Reengineering Federal Elections

This presentation highlights the fact that, in order to improve the outcomes of federal elections and increase confidence among elected officials, the electorate needs to elect ("hire") dispassionate problem solvers, not the most eloquent or those with the best platform.

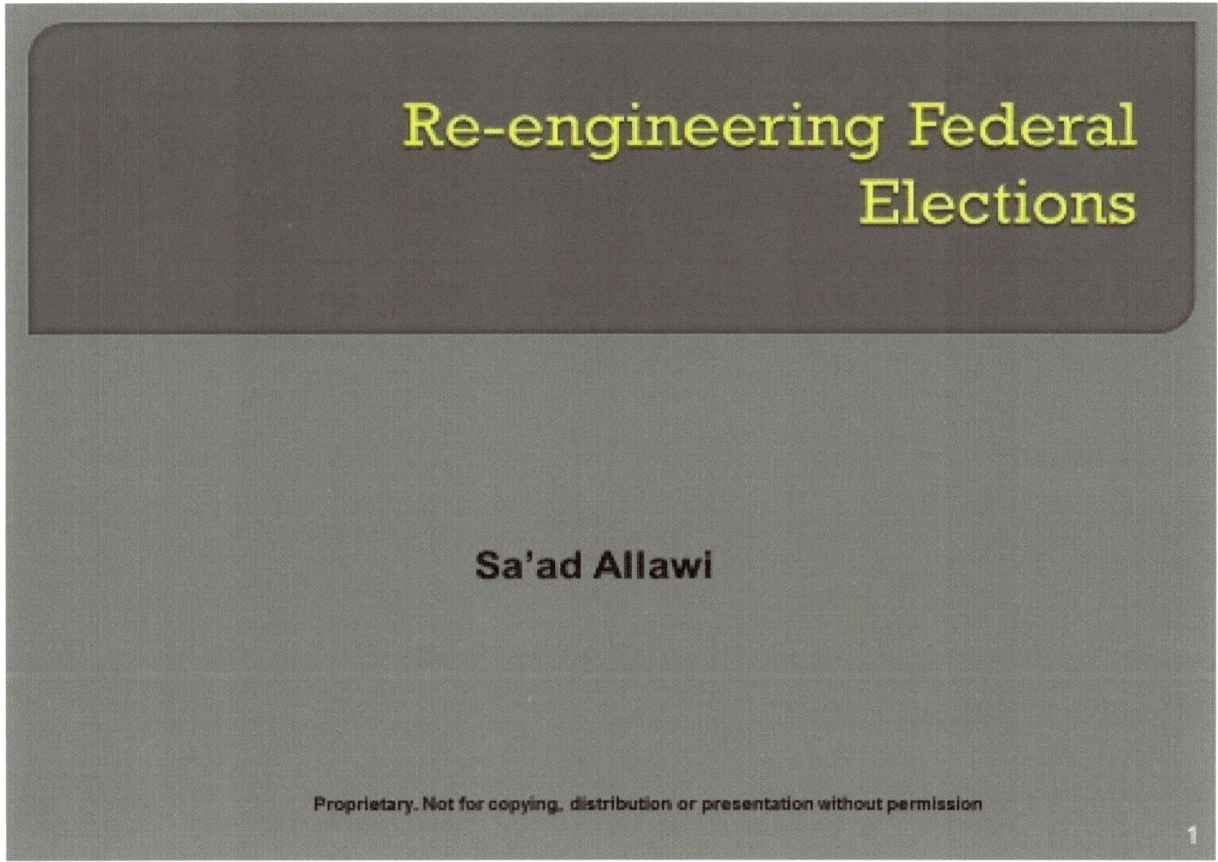

One of the reasons the U.S. has been declining is its ineffective federal elections, which is the subject of this chapter.

There are other issues such as the Government Bureaucracy and Federal Reserve which have little oversight. These are very important and may be the subject of presentations in due course.

This chapter also discusses the problems with elections today, utilizes McKinsey's 7-S framework to come up with suggested common sense solutions at the national level and what individuals can do to improve the outcome of elections and confidence in their officials, and discusses the "Job Interview" format that focuses on the candidate's resume instead of debating the candidate's platform and beliefs.

Today's discussion

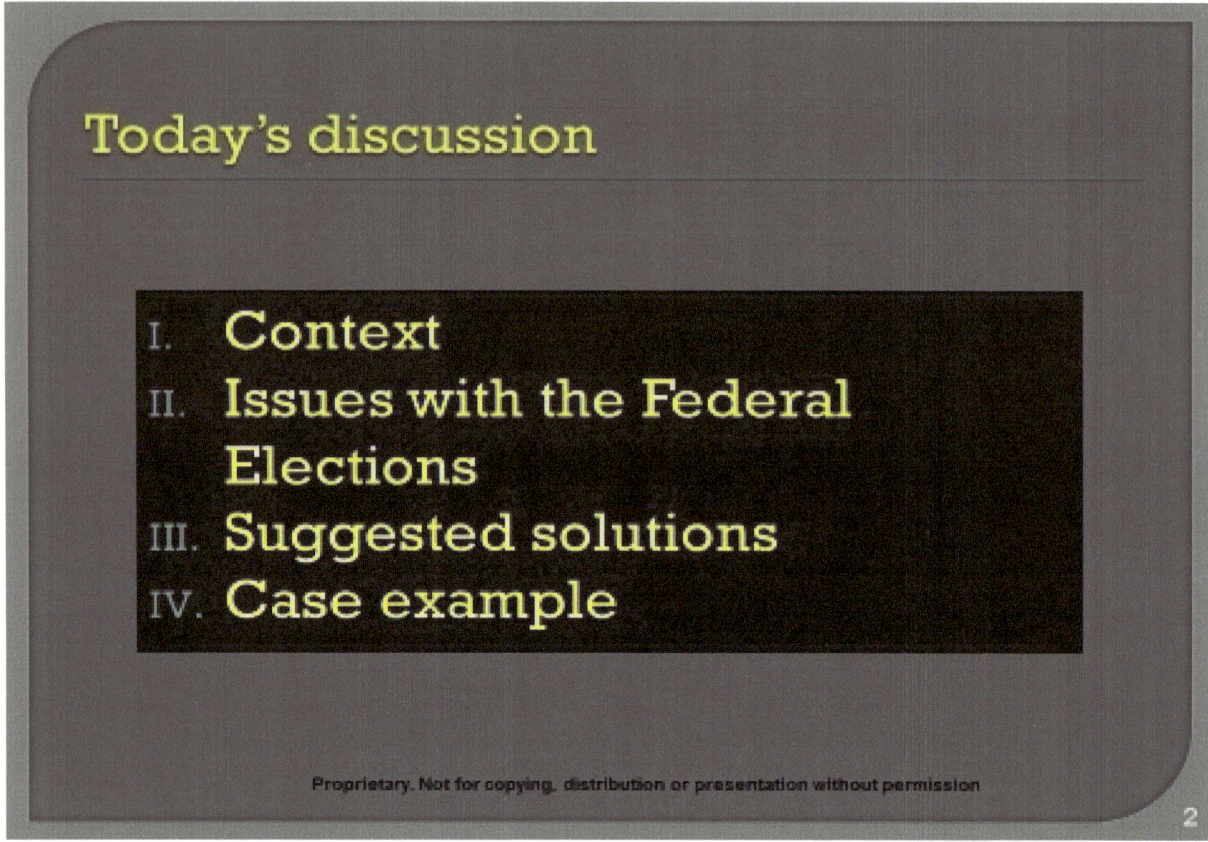

Today's discussion will cover the following:

- Context – How does this fit into the overall picture
- Issues with federal elections
- Suggested solutions based on sound management practices
- A case example from the author

I. Context – Unhappiness

- US has been in relative decline over the past few decades

- One reason - Ineffective Federal Government

3

The U.S. has been in relative decline in economic, fiscal, social and scientific terms over the past few decades – discussed in the prior presentation.

One of the reasons for this decline is the ineffective federal government. There are other reasons which relate to policy and strategy which are not discussed in this presentation.

I. Context – Election issues

- Federal, not state elections

- Limited to election issues

- "7-S" framework for excellence

- Sound management solutions

4

This presentation covers federal – not state – elections, although many of the items discussed here and recommendations will apply equally to state and local elections.

Some of the ideas presented also apply to elections in other western-style democracies.

It is limited only to election issues, not policy and strategy to reposition the U.S., which was discussed in the last chapter.

Lastly, it utilizes sound management solutions rather than political ones.

In Search of Excellence

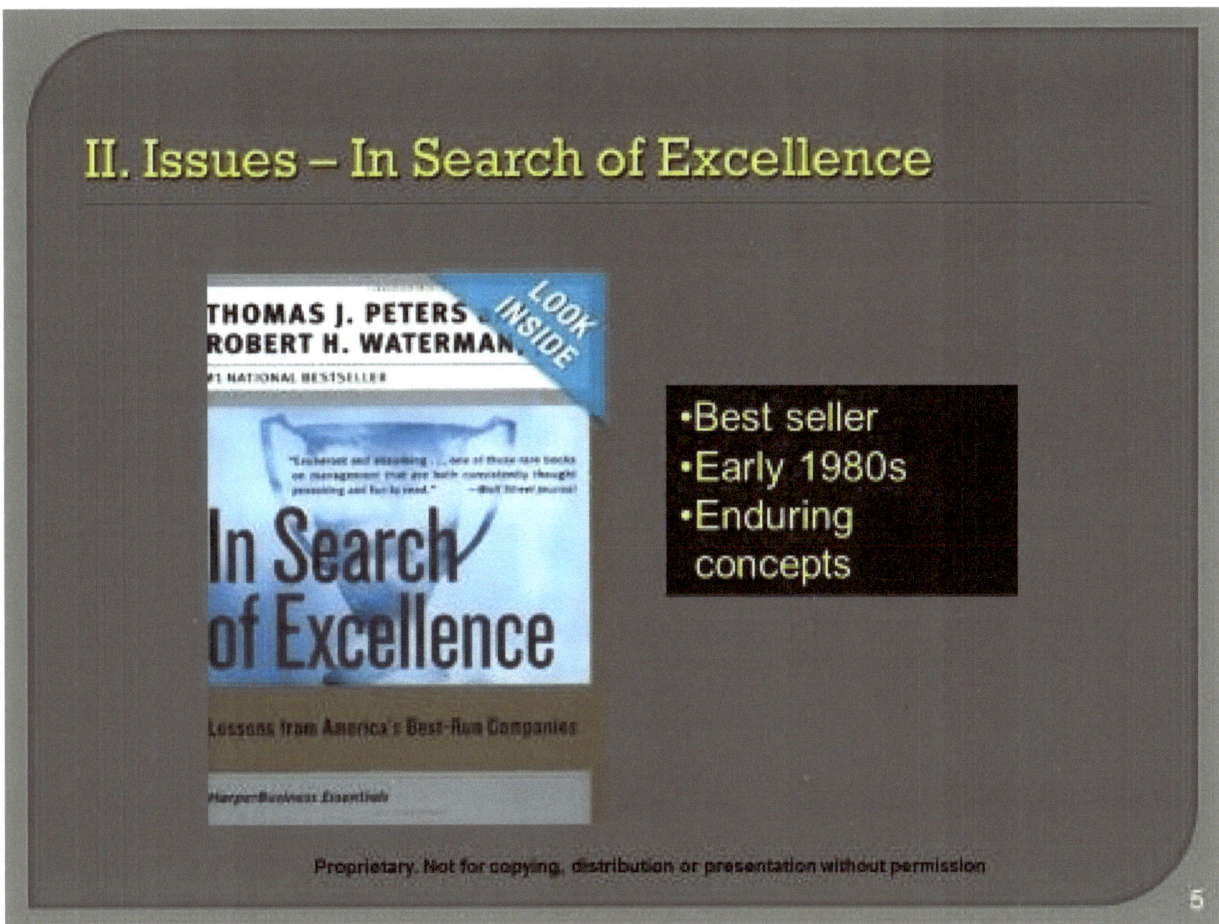

And again, I will use the 7-S template described in the best seller, <u>In Search of Excellence</u>.

The template that we will be using has seven S's.

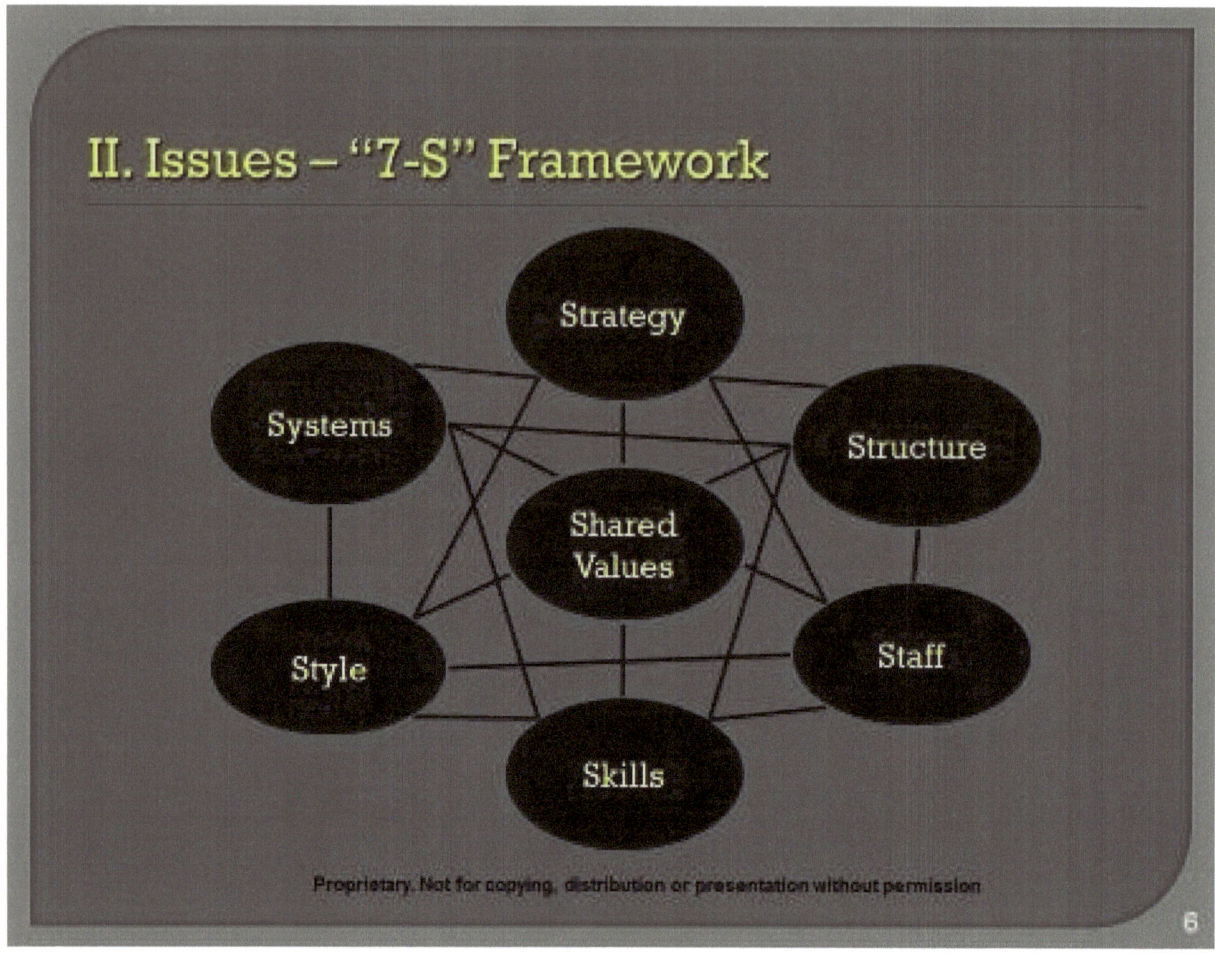

Starting in the middle, **Shared Values** refers to the mission; i.e. what is the mission of the organization?

At the twelve o'clock position is **Strategy**; i.e., how do you make your mission a reality?

Moving clockwise is **Structure**, which refers to the reporting relationships between people in an organization (lines and boxes) and accountability.

Next is **Staff** – How many people do you need to run the organization, of what type, and where are they located?

Skills – What are the core competencies required to run the organization?

Style – What management style is used (e.g. top-down or bottom-up, competitive or collaborative)?

Finally, **Systems** – Management, procedures, and practices as well as information technology systems.

Mission and strategy

II. Issues – Mission and Strategy

- Elected officials increasingly representing special interests and parties

- Politics has increasingly become a "profession" not a "calling"

- Officials beholden to the source of money

- Short rather than long term objectives

- Gerrymandering reduces free competition (14%)

Proprietary. Not for copying, distribution or presentation without permission

7

Elected officials are increasingly representing special interests and parties. This has become more pervasive in the past few decades. Politics has increasingly become a life-long goal. Many representatives go to Congress and stay for a long time, making it a profession, not a calling. This is inconsistent with the intent of the founding fathers. Elected officials are increasingly beholden to the source of money and power to help them get reelected. The source could be contributors or the party they belong to. They are increasingly thinking short-term (the next election cycle), not long-term. Furthermore, gerrymandering reduces free competition. Only 14% of all of the congressional districts in the United States are truly free. The other 86% are gerrymandered so that they're safe for one or the other party.

Structure and procedures in place in the U.S. are as follows:

II. Issues – Structure and Procedures

- Money wins elections

- Leadership of committees based on seniority

- Election process too long

- Debating process not helpful in identifying core competency for governing

- Elected officials underpaid compared to peers

8

"Money Wins Elections". The more you have to spend, the more likely you'll be elected.

Leadership of committees is based on seniority, not necessarily on competency or performance,

The elections process is too long. In Canada and the U.K., it is twelve weeks, while ours lasts up to 18 months.

The debating process is not helpful in identifying core competency for governing.

Elected officials are underpaid compared to their peers in the private and non-profit sectors. This is an important issue, because if you ask someone to do public service for six or eight years, you want to make sure at least that they do not lose compensation, especially since they will likely fall behind in their career track if they decide to serve.

Staff skills and styles:

The best and most qualified candidates are not interested in political service, because the process itself is very painful, and many of them don't think they can make a difference even if elected. Furthermore, officials are elected on promises, not performance and results. Winning is based on fundraising and networking competencies, not management ability. Blaming others or "kicking the can down the road" is a way to deflect problems and protect one's political career.

Debates have come to resemble horse racing, boxing matches, or gladiator events, with interest on winning rather than solving issues. Finally, poor performers stay in the job for a long time, and they're not accountable to the electorate.

What are the suggested solutions?

Shared values (mission).

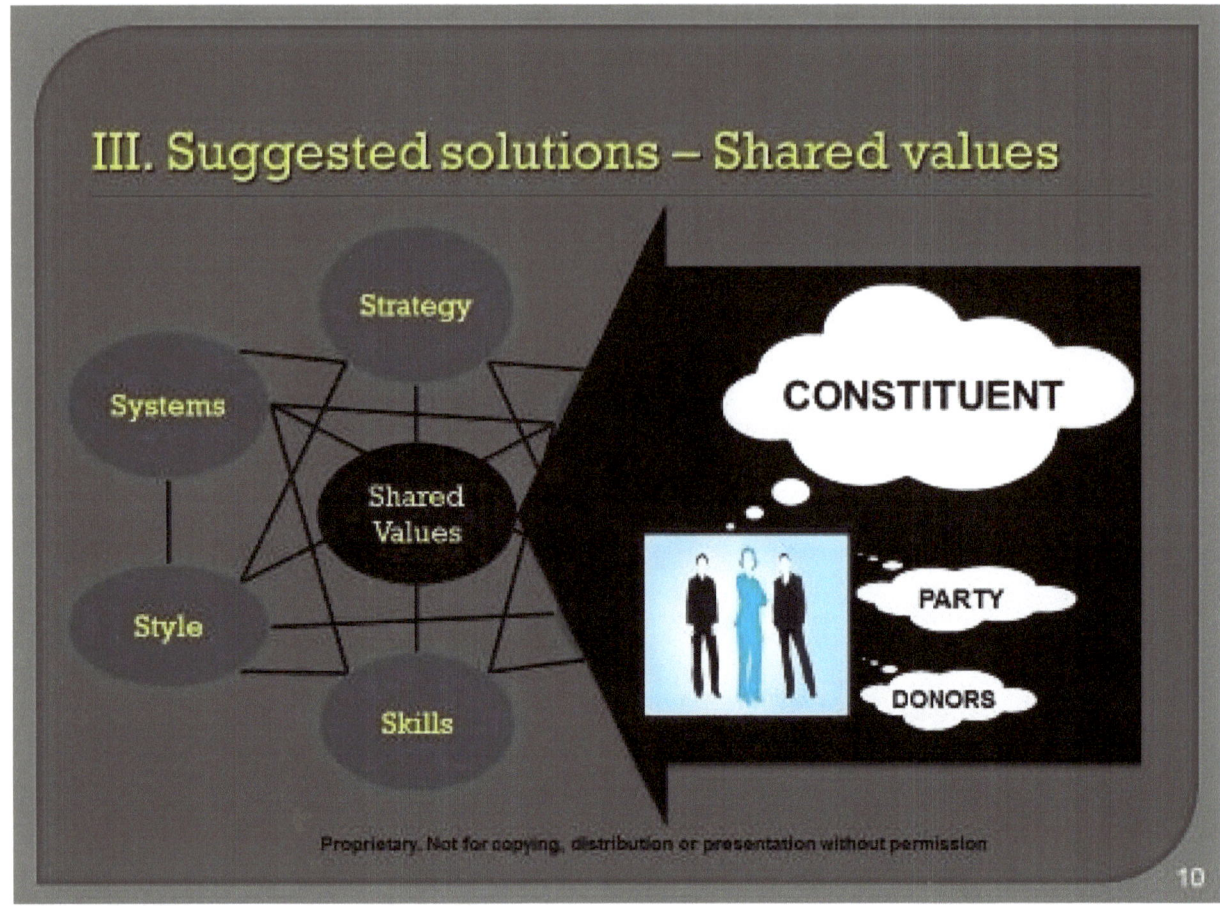

We would like to see our representatives represent mostly their constituents' will, and much less so their party, donors or special interests.

Representative refers to any elected official (Member of the House, Senator, or President). We need to have our representatives spend 60-70% of their time taking care of what their constituents want, instead of 60-70% of their time taking care of what their party or special interests want.

This is easier said than done. The other "S"s following help make that achievable.

The Rule of Seven and Accountability:

III. Suggested solutions – The rule of 7 and accountability

- "Any effect of organizational tenure on performance should be nonlinear:
  "…with a larger positive effect at low levels of tenure and with a diminishing effect as tenure increases"
  CAHRS

- A study in the 1970s – managers and executives add minimal value after 7 years tenure in the same job

- "President should be a 7 year term" – *Thomas Jefferson: The Art of Power*

- Retaining poor performers demoralizes others and reduces organization performance

Proprietary. Not for copying, distribution or presentation without permission

11

"Any effective organizational tenure on performance should be nonlinear, with a larger positive effect at low levels of tenure and with diminishing effect as tenure increases." This quote was developed by Cornell Advanced Human Resources Sciences (CAHRS). It indicates that an employee's contribution is most positive at the low level of tenure, and as their tenure increases, their contribution decreases.

A study in the early 1970s (I believe it was for Exxon Oil, but I'm not sure) concluded that managers and executives added minimal value after seven years of tenure in the same job. In support of this claim, Thomas Jefferson, during his presidency, was quoted as saying, "Presidency should be one seven-year term" - Thomas Jefferson, The Art of Power.

Jefferson, who lived 200+ years ago, and did not have the benefit of all the analysis that we have today, instinctively knew that if you spent more than seven years doing the same thing, your effectiveness wanes.

Finally, retaining poor performers demoralizes others and reduces the organization's overall performance.

The rule of seven

The rule of 7:

 There are 7 days of the week,

 7 heavens,

 7 deadly sins,

 7 seas,

 7 wonders of the world,

 7 colors of the rainbow,

 7 seals,

 7 habits of highly effective people,

 7 pillars of wisdom,

 Among others.

Why seven? Well, studies have shown that human beings are most effective at managing seven items at one time, and no more.

Thus., after seven years, a person's contribution becomes minimal, and it is very hard to manage more than seven items, **so it is logical to have term limits around the number seven.**

Strategy

One six-year term for President

One six-year term for senators (one-third of the Senate rolls over, as practiced today)

Eight years (two four-year terms) for House members. Two four-year terms – as opposed to four two-year terms – for House members provide more time for members to serve their constituents rather than spending time campaigning to get re-elected. If a House Representative is

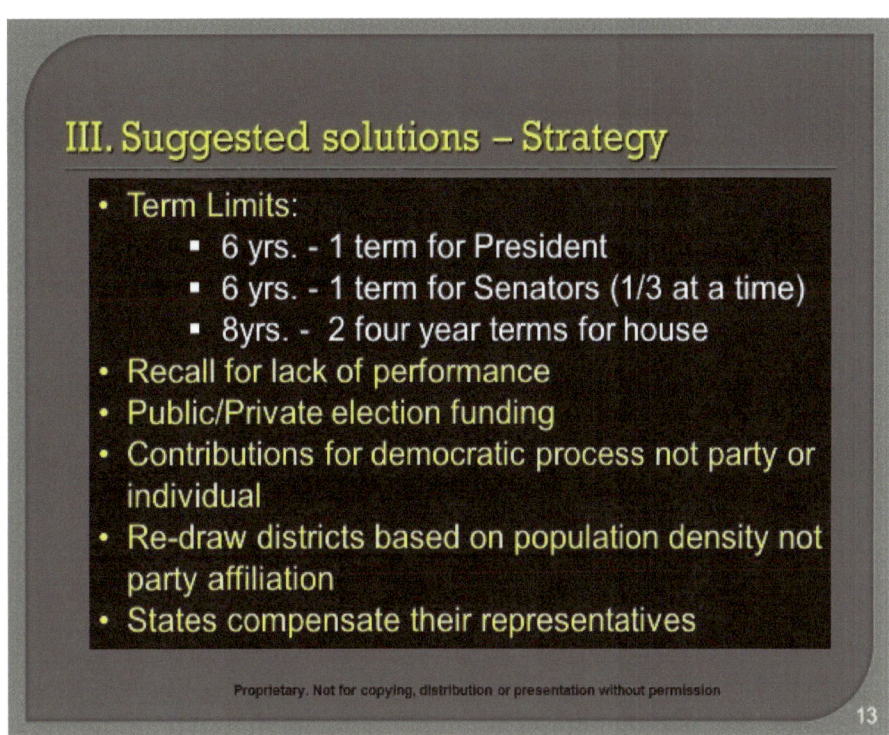

provided with a four-year term, he/she feels safe. In order to ensure that they perform, we need the ability to recall them for lack of performance, just like they do in the private sector.

Public-private election funding:

In the U.K., elections are publicly funded. Here in the U.S., It is mostly privately funded. To help ensure that elected officials represent the will of their electorates, not special interests, we need to change the source and structure of funding elections. As such, public-private funding makes sense. The funding needs to ensure that contributions go towards the democratic process, not a party or individual. The elected officials' behavior may change to serve the electorate, not the person or organization giving them the contribution.

We should then redraw the districts based on population density, not party affiliation. The districts need to be truly competitive, not safe for one party or the other, as they are today.

Finally, states should compensate their federal representatives. If you send somebody to Congress and they are paid by the state that they represent, they are much more likely to serve the people of that state.

Structure, staff, and skills:

III. Suggested solutions – Structure, Staff, Skills

- "Job interview" model replaces debates

- Election cycle limited to 3 – 6 months

- Committee leaders selected on performance not seniority

- Competency assessed based on experience not platform

14

Job interview format must replace debates. This idea will be discussed in more detail in subsequent slides.

Election cycle time should be limited to three to six months, not 18.

Committee leaders should be selected based on performance and competency, not seniority.

Competency should be assessed based on experience, not platform.

Systems:

III. Suggested solutions – Systems

- Compensate representatives on par with peers in private sector – salary plus incentive based on goals:
  - President – CEO of a large multi-national
  - Senators – senior partners in law firms
  - Representatives – junior partners in law firms
- Compensation tied to quantifiable goals
- Benefits during service – similar to the rest of the population:
  - Healthcare
  - Retirement pension

15

We must consider compensating elected officials on par with their peers in the private or non-profit sector. This means salary plus incentive, based on quantifiable goals or Management by Objectives (MBOs) tied to appropriate national performance goals similar to the ones mentioned in Chapter 1.

The President should get compensation equivalent to that of a CEO of a large multi-national corporation, Senators should be paid equivalent to a senior partner in law firms, and House Representatives' compensation should be equivalent to junior partners in law firms.

Why? The reasoning behind this claim relates to an earlier point. If you want competent individuals to serve, they should be compensated appropriately, because they will fall behind in their current career.

Incentive compensation should be tied to quantifiable goals and may be much larger than their salary if the goals are met.

Benefits during service should be similar to those of their peers in the population at large. Such benefits include healthcare and retirement.

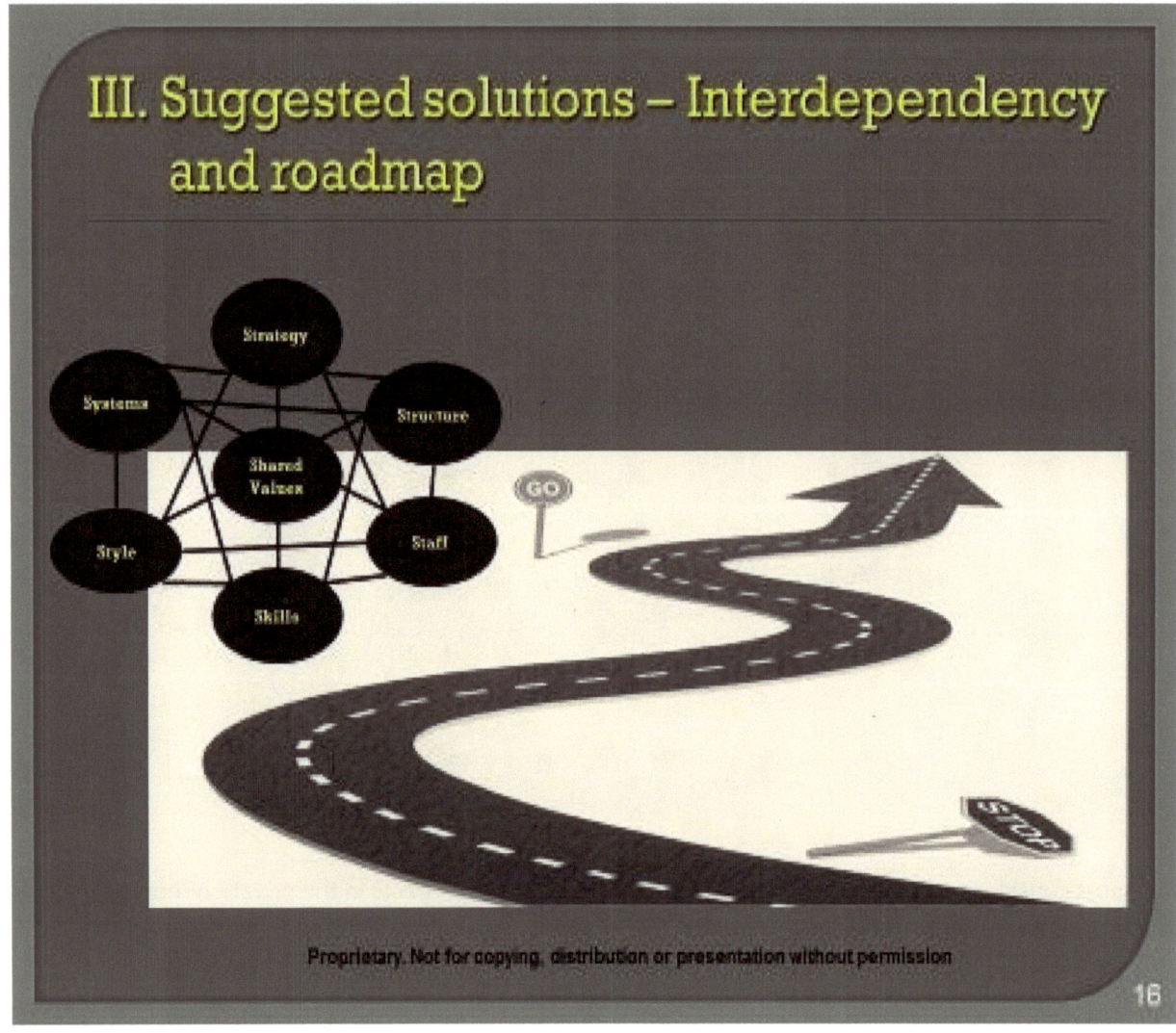

As mentioned earlier in this presentation when discussing the 7-S framework, the suggested solutions are interdependent.

All components of the 7-S model are interdependent, which means the changes have to fit together. Given that it is **difficult to make all the changes at the same time**, a road map for implementation is needed. We start with one change, then another and another. The election system in this country has become ineffective slowly over a long period of time. As such, it will be difficult to turn it around quickly, but we can turn it around faster than it took to get to this point. A ten-year roadmap for turning around the election system may be appropriate.

Suggested solutions on strategy:

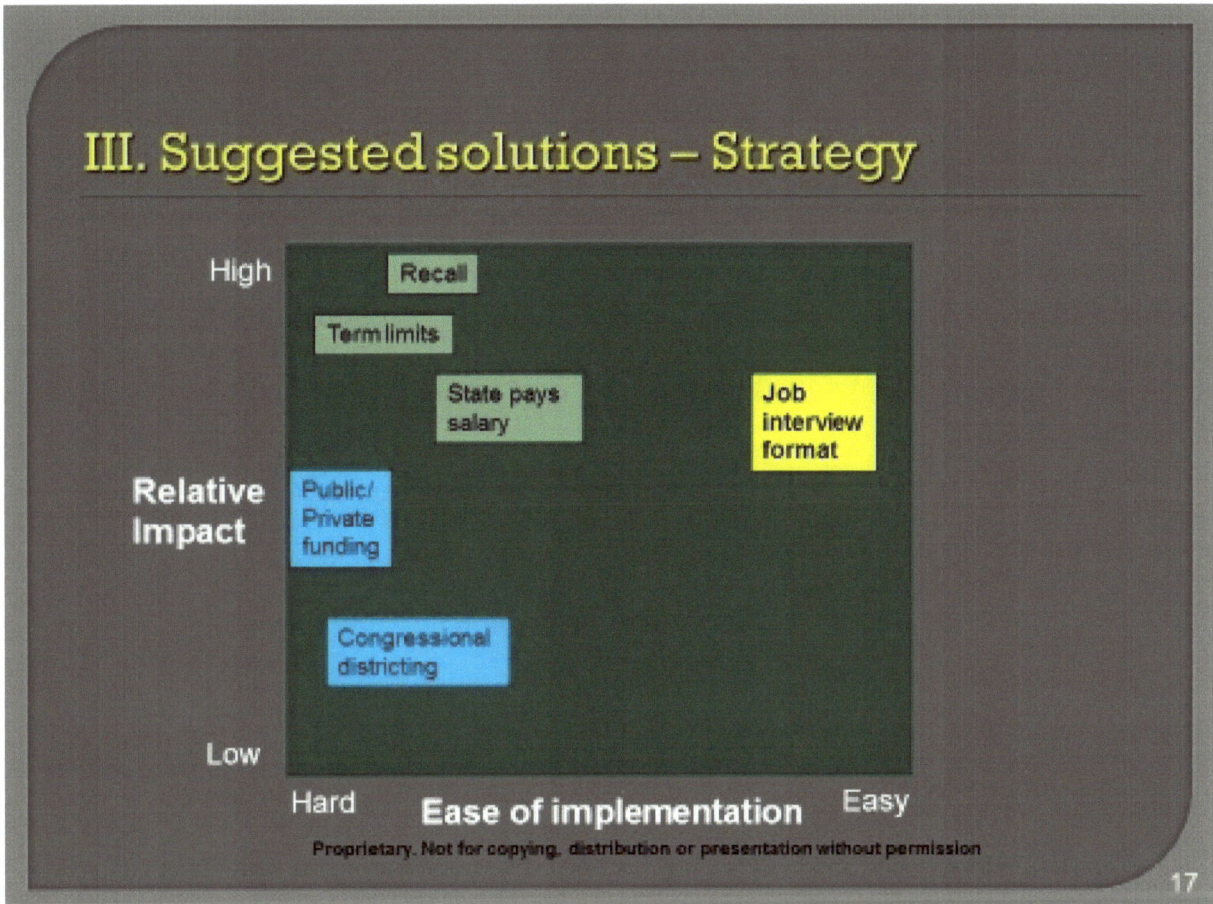

The matrix above summarizes the changes needed to restructure the federal election system. The "Y" axis shows the relative impact on election results from low to high. The "X" axis shows ease of implementation from hard to easy.

Some of the suggestions that were mentioned earlier are as follows:

The three items in green (recall federal elected official for lack of performance, have term limits, have state pay salary of federal official) all have a relatively high impact, but are also relatively hard (with varying degrees) to implement. These may be earlier contenders in the roadmap.

The two in blue (public-private funding and congressional redistricting) are relatively hard to apply, and their impact is a little lesser than the other ones. These may be later contenders for the roadmap,

Finally, the job interview format (In yellow) is the easiest to implement and has a relatively high impact – and should be adopted now.

Job interview format

What does the job interview format look like?
One candidate is examined at a time.

The electorate submit or ask questions, which are selected randomly. The job of the moderator is to make sure that the meeting process is under control not ask questions.

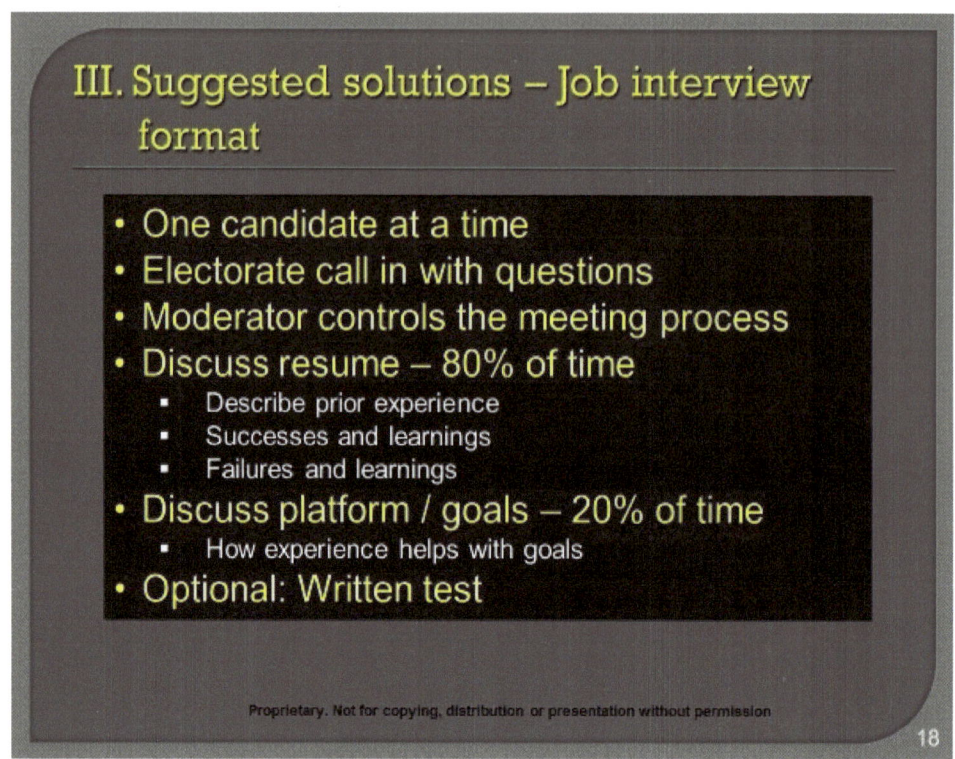

Candidates and electorate discuss the resume 80% of the time. The candidate describes his/her prior experience; what were his/her successes and what did he/she learn from them, what were his/her failures and what was learned from them?

Discussion should touch on the candidate's platform and goals, comprising the remaining 20% of the interview. The candidate should be asked to articulate how his/her prior experience can help to achieve his/her goals.

Finally, the candidate might take a written test, something that can be done further down-the-road.

> When I have presented this slide to live audiences in the past, I ask the question, *"How many of you have actually hired people for jobs?"* Some portion of the audience puts their hand up. Then I ask, *"How many of those with your hands up have hired individuals based on their performance in debating other finalists for the job?"* Members of the audience all laugh.

The point is this: When considering hiring (electing) individuals, you want to look at their resume and experience and how their resume and prior experience will help them succeed in meeting their goals. Spend most of the interview discussing their resume, not their platform, because they can't deliver on the platform. The political system is a very large and complicated machine that is a hindrance to deliver on the platform.

Plato said it best

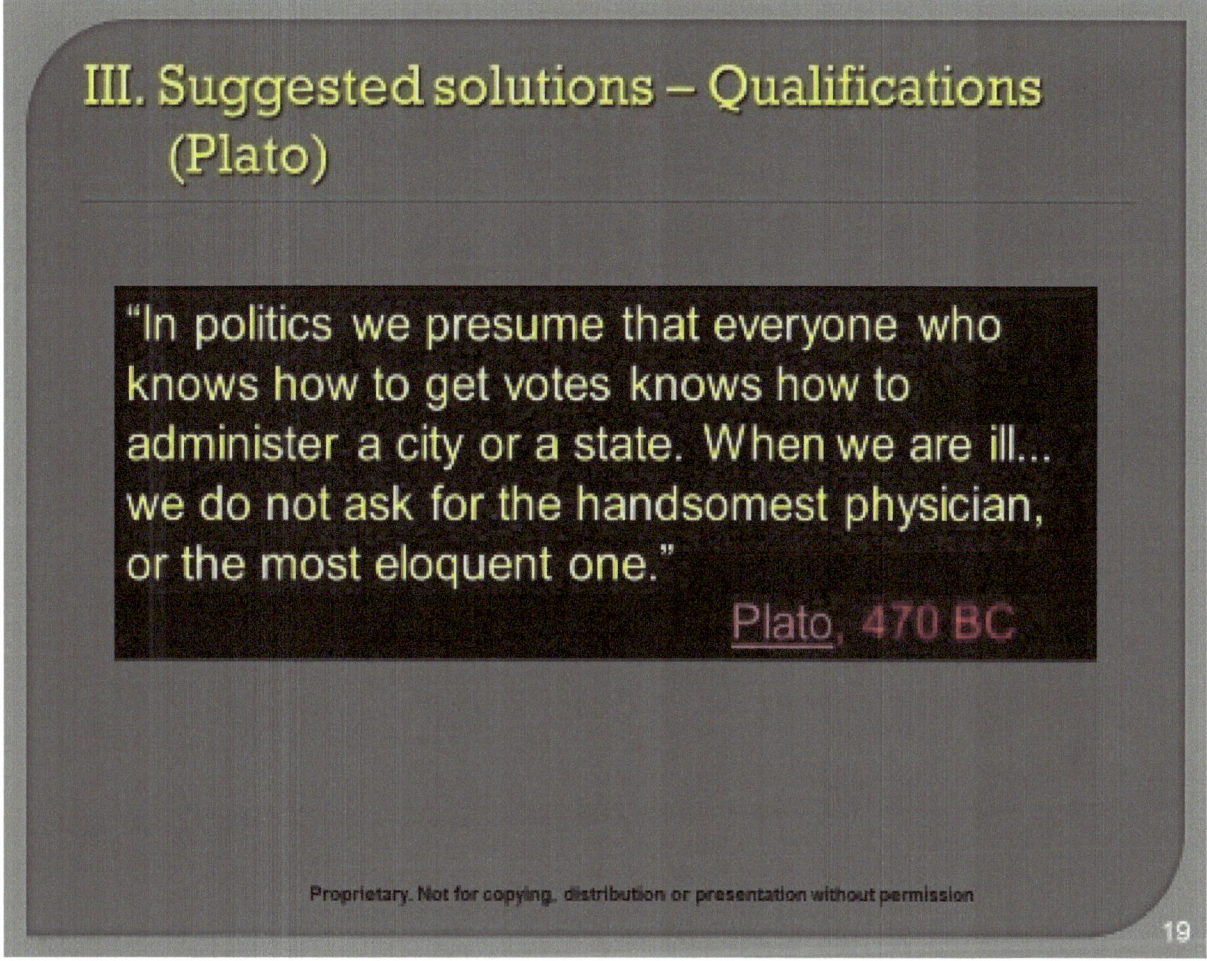

And by the way, there is somebody else who articulated the issue of electing officials with the wrong set of skills better than I did:

Plato said in 470 BC, *"In politics we presume that everyone who knows how to get votes knows how to administer a city or a state. When we are ill, we do not ask for the handsomest physician or the most eloquent one."*

If you are going to hire (elect) someone, do so based on his or her track record. Past experience can help an individual get the job done well. Do not hire (elect) someone who makes the biggest promises, has the best platform, is the most eloquent, or is the most charismatic. After all, we have been electing people on that basis for the past 40 years, and where has it gotten U.S.?

Voting process (very similar to the hiring process):

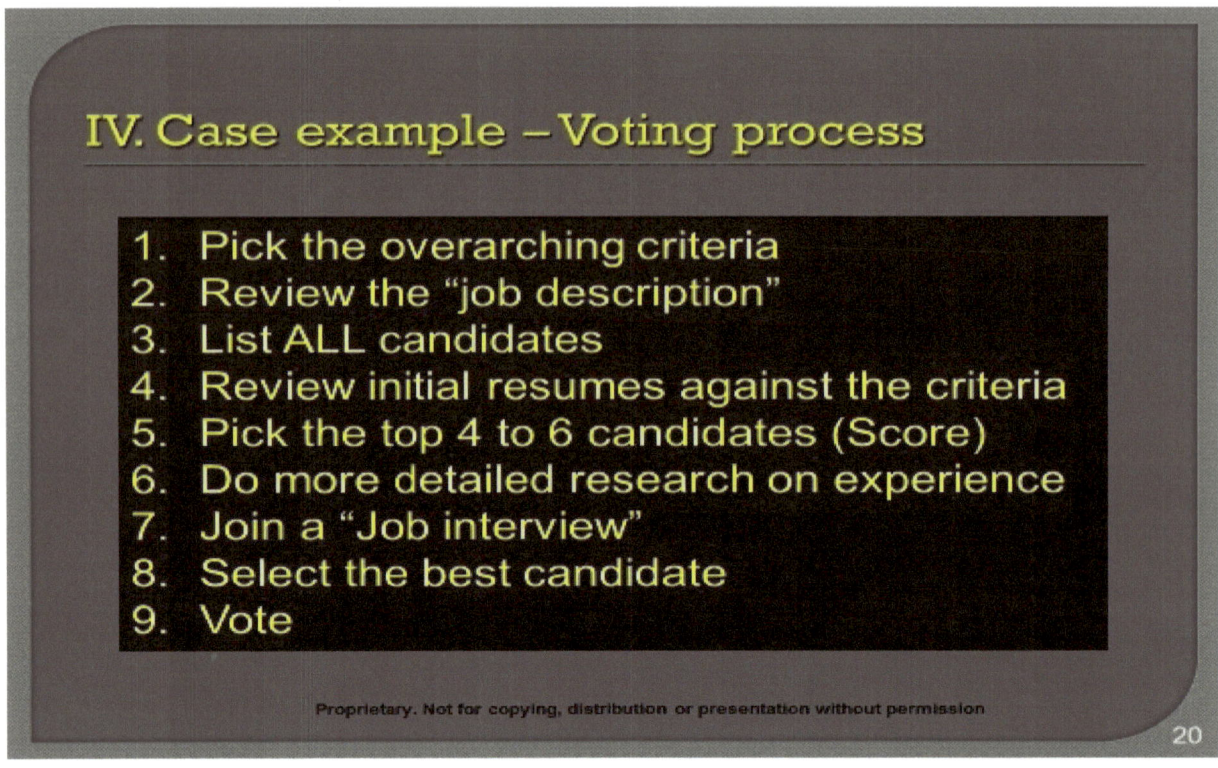

IV. Case example – Voting process

1. Pick the overarching criteria
2. Review the "job description"
3. List ALL candidates
4. Review initial resumes against the criteria
5. Pick the top 4 to 6 candidates (Score)
6. Do more detailed research on experience
7. Join a "Job interview"
8. Select the best candidate
9. Vote

20

Pick the overarching criteria, just like a job specification/description.

Review the job description for the candidate. There are "job descriptions" on government websites for President, Senator, and House Representative. The descriptions don't tell you what a candidate's experience should be, but they tell you what the job responsibilities are.

Then list **ALL** the candidates who are running for that position. Just like when you're advertising for a job, you get a number of resumes, you look through all the resumes, and then you pick the top one. Do not restrict yourself to a particular party, as you may lose more suitable candidates in another party.

Review initial resumes/bios (available on the candidate's website or other websites) against your overarching criteria, and score each candidate from 1 to 10 (1 is the least likely to meet your criteria and 10 is the highest),

Pick the top three to four candidates based on the scores given. Do more detailed analysis on the remaining candidates' experience using the Internet. If you are hiring somebody for a job, this is probably where you call the prior employer or another source for a reference.

Have the candidate come in for a job interview (described earlier). If the job interview format cannot take place, rely on the steps above to choose. Do not get enamored by the candidate's debating skills.

Select the best candidate and vote.

For all of U.S. who have hired employees previously, the election process should be very similar to the hiring process.

For example, criteria for president:

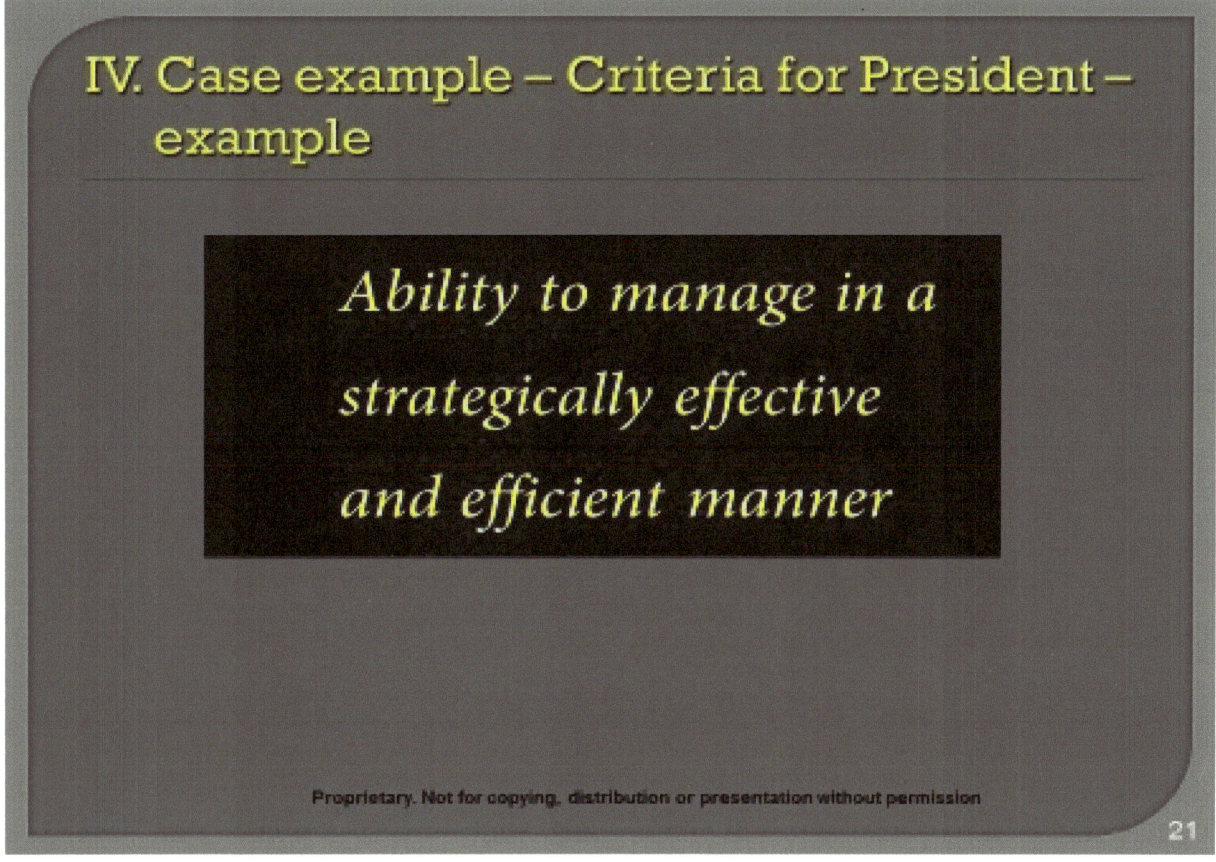

IV. Case example – Criteria for President – example

Ability to manage in a strategically effective and efficient manner

Proprietary. Not for copying, distribution or presentation without permission

21

My personal criterion for president is "the ability to manage in a strategically effective and efficient manner."

Criteria are different for every different person. Yours may include socially liberal, socially conservative, fiscally liberal, fiscally conservative, trustworthy, or any other characteristics.

Some of the criteria that people often pick are "most likely to win, affiliation with Party X or Party Y." In that case, we do not need to consider the resume, because the most-likely-to-win person is the person who has done best in the debates and has generated the highest polls.

> **If you vote for someone based on his or her debating performance or poll numbers and are later disappointed when he/she does not deliver on those promises, you should award yourself the "Plato Award."**

Takeaways on reengineering elections:

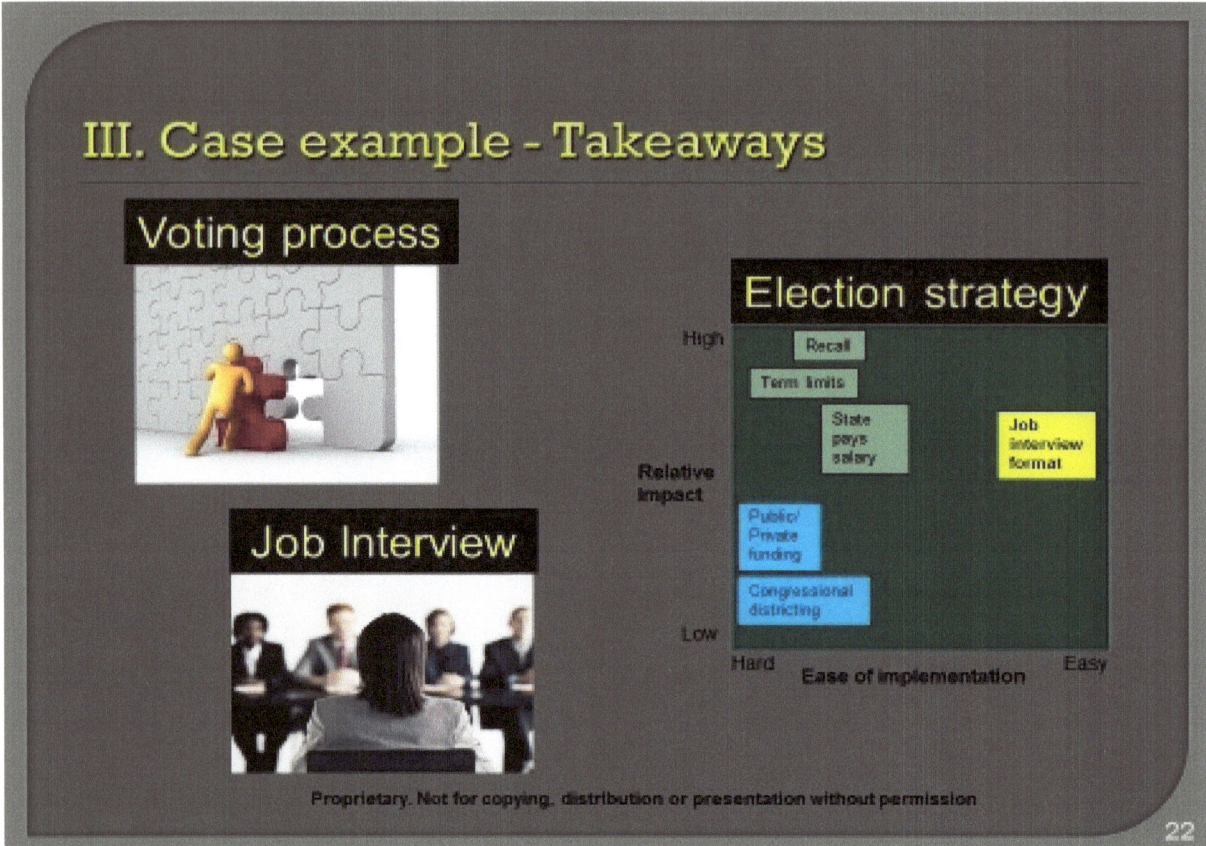

Insist on having a voting process that is similar to a hiring process.

Ensure that, over time, the election strategies (as described earlier) are put in place to help make the election system more effective.

Push the job interview format (that's one of the simplest things to do).

Why is this relevant? Since 2005, over 50% (over 80% by 2016) of the people of this country have been unhappy with Congress' performance. Similarly, since 2003, 58% (over 75% by 2016) of the people think the country is heading in the wrong direction. If we keep voting the same way, we will get the same outcome.

Albert Einstein's definition of insanity is *"Doing the same thing over and over and expecting a different outcome."* This perfectly describes our process of electing our officials.

> *In my case, I've been voting independently for the past five general elections. I have never voted for a Presidential candidate who has won office in that period, because every time I vote, I pick my criteria and I pick the most qualified candidate for those criteria. That doesn't happen to be the person who wins; the winner is frequently the most charismatic candidate.*

Chapter 3

Healthcare: Avoiding the crisis of an enabling industry

This presentation provides a top-down and bottom-up system in which healthcare cost goals are established at the federal level, and workable solutions for reducing the costs are achieved at the state level by the practitioners in the industry.

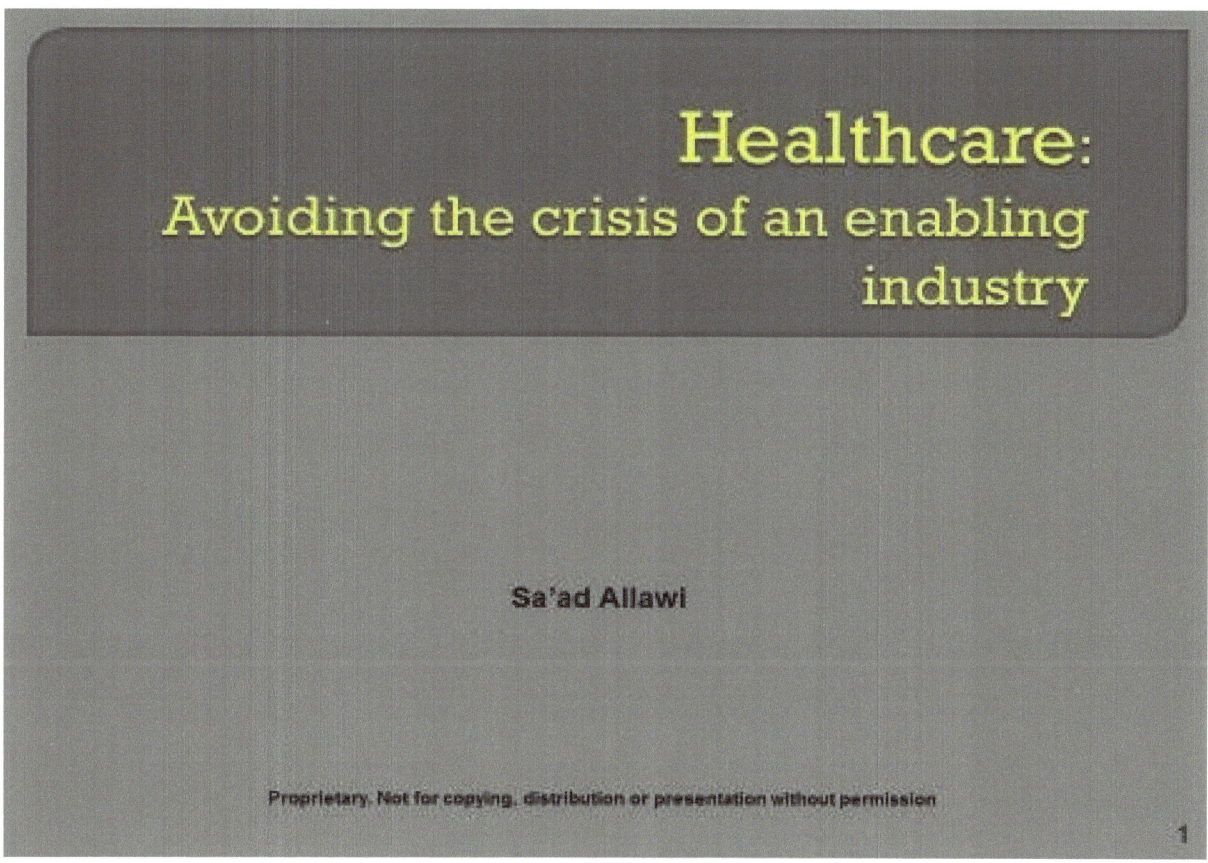

This presentation discusses healthcare costs as a major destabilizing influence in the U.S. This presentation also compares healthcare to the financial services industry, discusses the root causes of the cost problem, compares U.S. to other countries, and compares states with each other. It discusses the bottom-up approach to reducing costs at the state level. This presentation is based on a white paper written in 2009 that has been updated regularly since then. It takes a strategic look at healthcare costs and provides an approach for operational solutions. It does not address Obamacare.

The agenda of this presentation covers four items

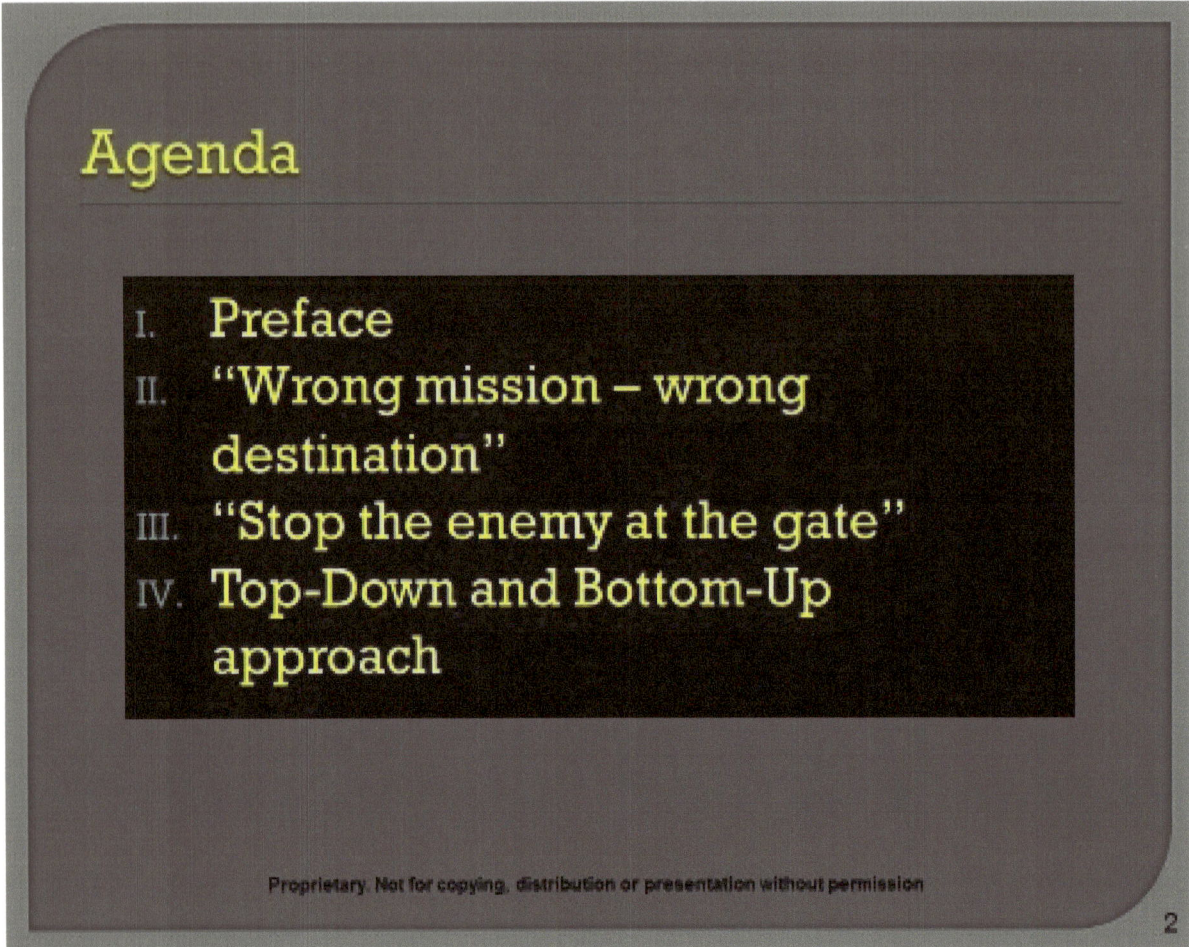

The preface of this presentation – crystalizing a mission gone awry of an enabling industry

The wrong mission and the wrong destination for healthcare

How to "stop the enemy at the gate", to mitigate a very likely crisis

And a top-down and bottom-up approach for fixing healthcare costs

Preface

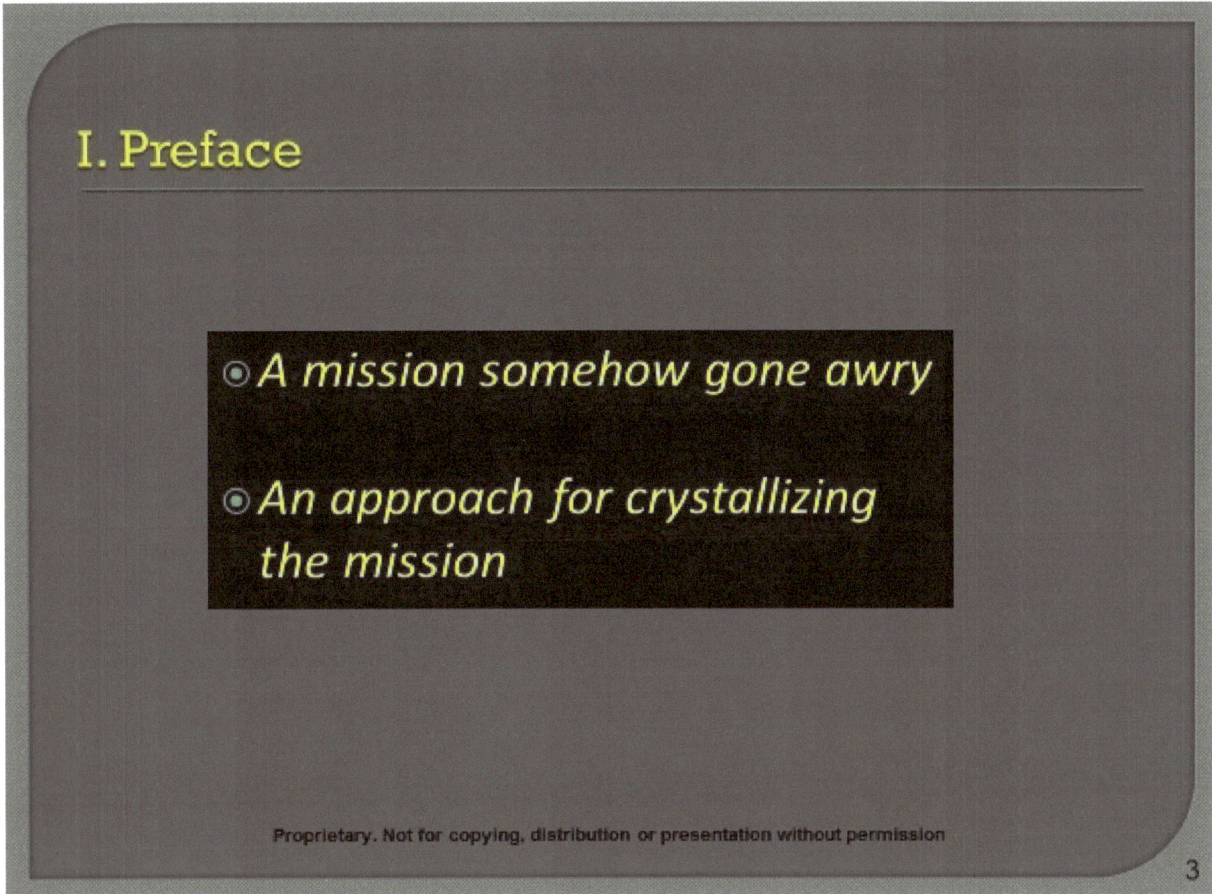

I. Preface

- *A mission somehow gone awry*

- *An approach for crystallizing the mission*

Proprietary. Not for copying, distribution or presentation without permission

3

The mission of the healthcare industry, which is an enabling industry, has gone awry. This presentation discussed an approach for crystalizing the mission and re-establishing the direction of the healthcare industry.

II. Wrong mission – Enabling industries

⊙ *Enabling industries:* Industries which make other industries, businesses and individuals more productive, e.g.:

- Financial Services
- Healthcare
- Government agencies

⊙ *Crisis:* wrong mission – focus on own their growth rather than enable

Proprietary. Not for copying, distribution or presentation without permission

4

Enabling industries are industries that make other industries, businesses, and individuals more productive. For example, the financial services industry provides money for growth, investment, and building businesses; the healthcare industry provides services to individuals so they can remain healthy and be productive; and government agencies provide infrastructure so that businesses and individuals can build. A crisis occurs when these enabling industries establish the wrong mission, such as focusing on their own growth, rather than enabling other industries and other individuals to grow.

II. Wrong mission – Financial services industry

- 20 to 30 years ago, the Financial services industry was true to its enabling mission

- Since then factors altered the industry's mission

- Financial industry began to generate profits in its own products

- A boom ensued as a result of growth which was faster than overall GDP

- Reached 20.7% of GDP in 2007 and collapsed in 2008

5

Let's look at the example of financial services, which presents a recent and vivid problem.

Twenty to thirty years ago, the financial industry was true to its enabling mission. It provided money for investments. Since then, many factors have altered the industry mission. That includes regulation, deregulation, and combining different parts of the industry (e.g., investment, commercial, and retail). The financial services industry began to generate profit in its own products; e.g. derivatives and mortgage-backed securities. These products began to make money for the industry itself. The result was rapid growth of the financial services industry – faster than the growth of the overall gross domestic product (GDP).

As a result of this differential growth, the industry reached 20.7% of GDP in 2007 and collapsed in 2008.

II. Wrong mission – Healthcare following suit

- Healthcare industry enabled people by keeping them healthy and productive

- Over the years the mission has faded and morphed

- The result caused healthcare to profit in its own products

- Healthcare costs grew at 6.6% annually, higher than GDP growth of 3.8%

- Healthcare accounted for 17.5% of GDP in 2014

6

Wrong mission, wrong destination; healthcare is following in the same footsteps of the financial services industry. The healthcare industry previously enabled people by keeping them healthy and productive so that they can add value and build wealth. Over the years, the mission has faded and morphed. Healthcare began to profit from its own product; hospitals grew in patient volume, and providers avoided high-risk patients and increased the intake of low-risk patients. Medicare was prohibited from negotiating volume discounts with pharmaceutical companies in spite of the fact that the drugs sold in the U.S. can be obtained at a much lower price internationally.

This push to grow caused the healthcare industry to generate profits. The industry grew at 6.6% annually over ten years – higher than the overall gross domestic product growth of 3.8%. By 2014, healthcare accounted for 17.5% of the GDP.

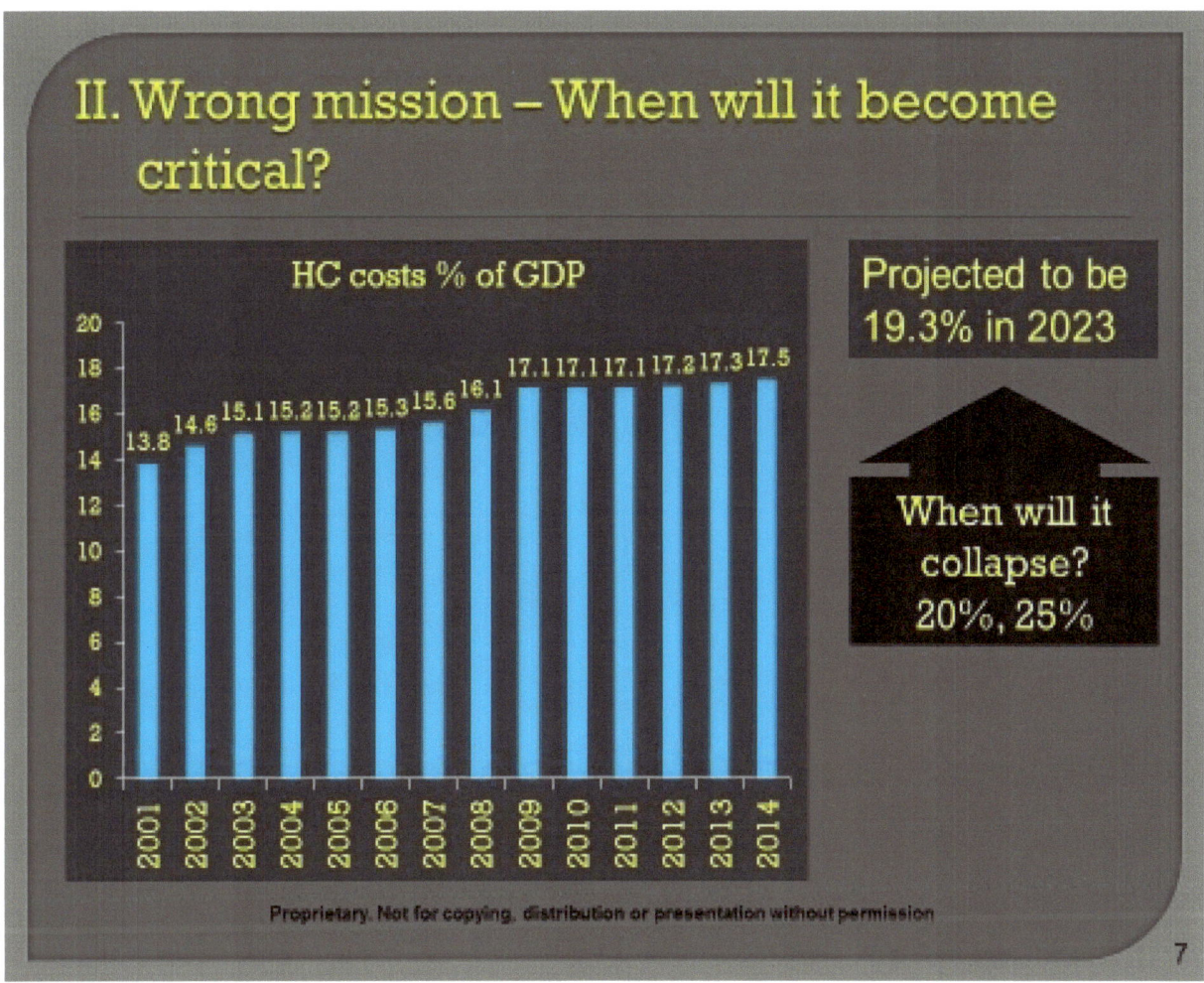

Healthcare costs as a percentage of the GDP rose from 15% in 2001 to 17.5% in 2014. It is projected to be 19.3% of the GDP in 2023. So when will it collapse? At 20% or 25%? If this trend continues, it will face the same fate as the financial services industry.

We must "stop the enemy at the gate."

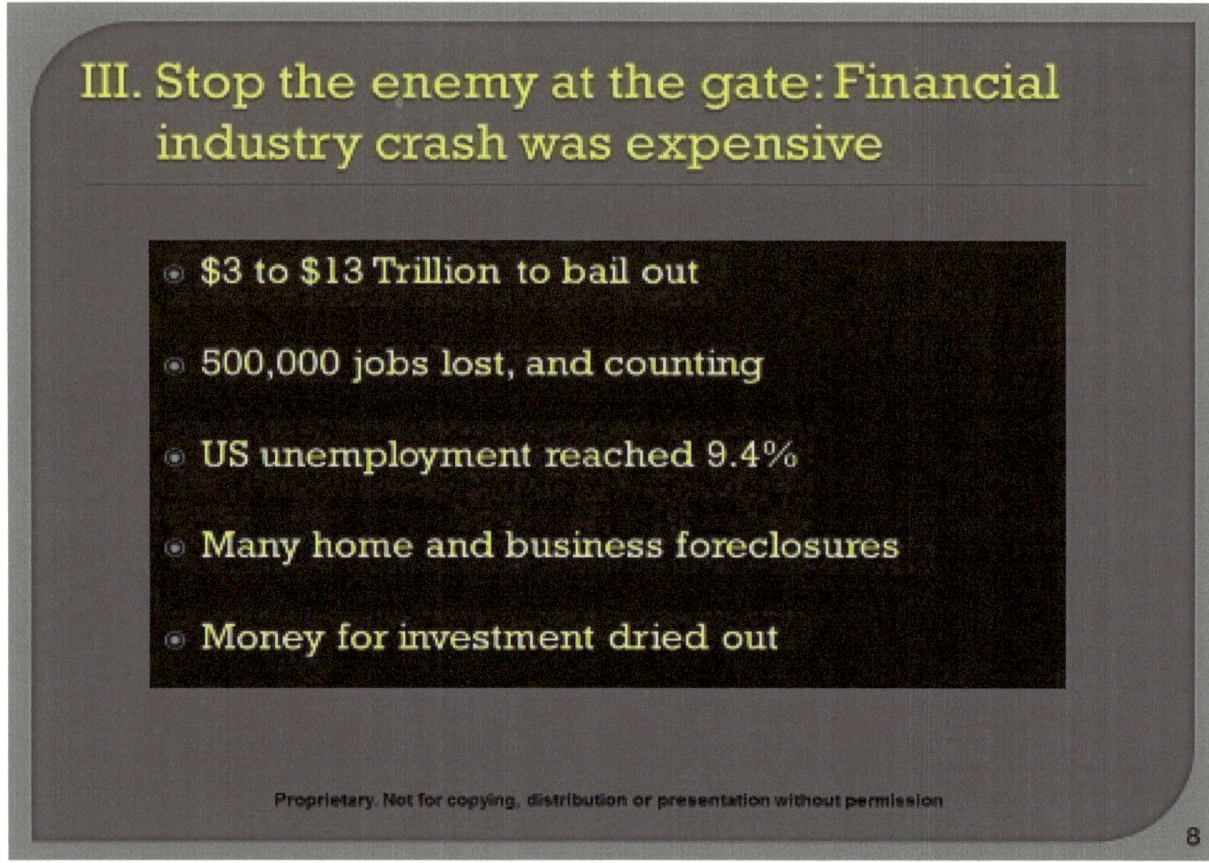

The bailout after the financial services crash was very expensive (estimated to be between $3 trillion and $13 trillion), including cleaning toxic assets and bailing out industries that suffered as a result; e.g. the automobile Industry. Five hundred thousand people (and counting) lost their jobs. U.S. unemployment reached 9.4% during the peak of the crisis. Many homes and businesses were foreclosed on, and money for investment dried up.

Healthcare is bigger than financial services

III. Stop the enemy at the gate: Healthcare is bigger and more pervasive

- $3.1 Trillion in current expenditure (2014)
- Approx. 16 million (+) workers vs. 8 in the Financial Industry
- Approx. 600,000 establishments many more than the Financial Industry
- Every community in the US – major employer in many

Proprietary. Not for copying, distribution or presentation without permission

9

The problem with the healthcare industry is that it's much bigger and more pervasive than the financial services industry. Healthcare expenditures were $3.1 trillion in 2014. It employs approximately 16 plus million individuals, versus 8 million in the financial services industry. There are approximately 600,000 healthcare establishments – many more than the financial industry, and finally, it impacts every community in the U.S., especially those in which healthcare is the major employer. By contrast, the financial services industry is concentrated in a few cities and towns.

III. Stop the enemy at the gate: Healthcare collapse would be greater

- 10 to 30% of payers might become bankrupt

- 10 to 30% of healthcare providers might go out of business

- Large unemployment especially in provider intensive areas

- Many consumers will end up without adequate care

- Massive bailout would be required – larger than the Financial Industry one

10

If the healthcare industry reached a crisis and faced collapse, the results would be far worse than those of the financial services industry collapse. 10 to 30% of payers (insurance companies, HMOs, and others) would likely go bankrupt, and 10 to 30% of healthcare providers would also likely go out of business. That's especially true in rural communities where these providers are major employers. And because they are major employers, the result would be serious unemployment in each of those communities. Furthermore, many consumers could end up without adequate care. Furthermore, massive bailout would be required—larger than that of the financial service industry. There is probably not enough discretionary funds in the world to fix the healthcare industry if it collapsed.

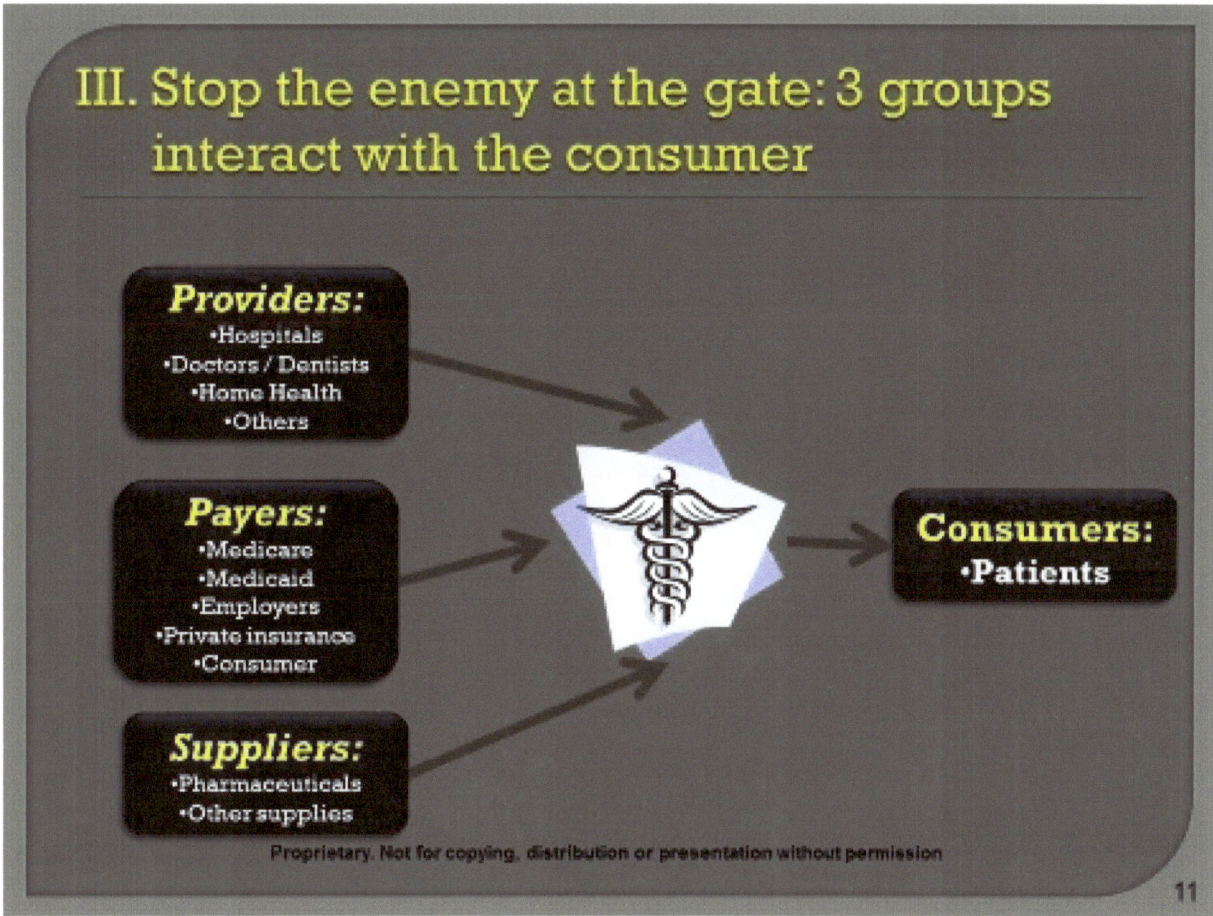

The structure of the industry is complicated. Three groups interact with the consumer/patient in healthcare:

- Providers (hospitals, doctors, dentists, home health, and others)
- Payers (Medicare, Medicaid, employer private insurance and consumers)
- Suppliers (pharmaceuticals, devices, general supplies, and others)

U.S. healthcare costs are high

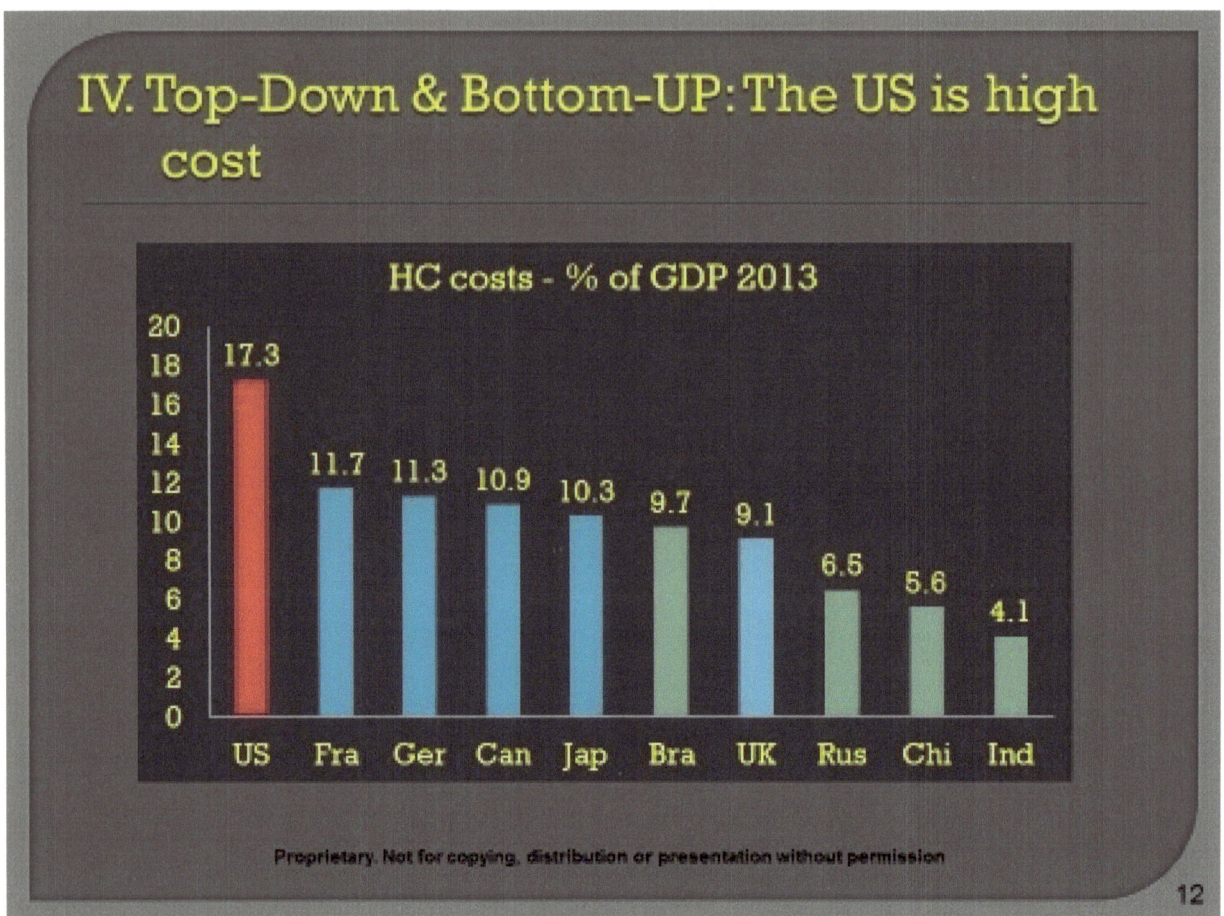

The U.S. has high healthcare costs in terms of percentage of GDP (17.3%) compared to other industrialized countries, whose percentages are as follows: France is at 11.7%, Germany 11.3%, Canada 10.9%, Japan 10.3%, and U.K. 9.1%.

The BRIC countries' percentages are even lower: Brazil is 9.7%, Russia is 6.5%, China is 5.6%, and India is 4.1.

Top-down and bottom-up

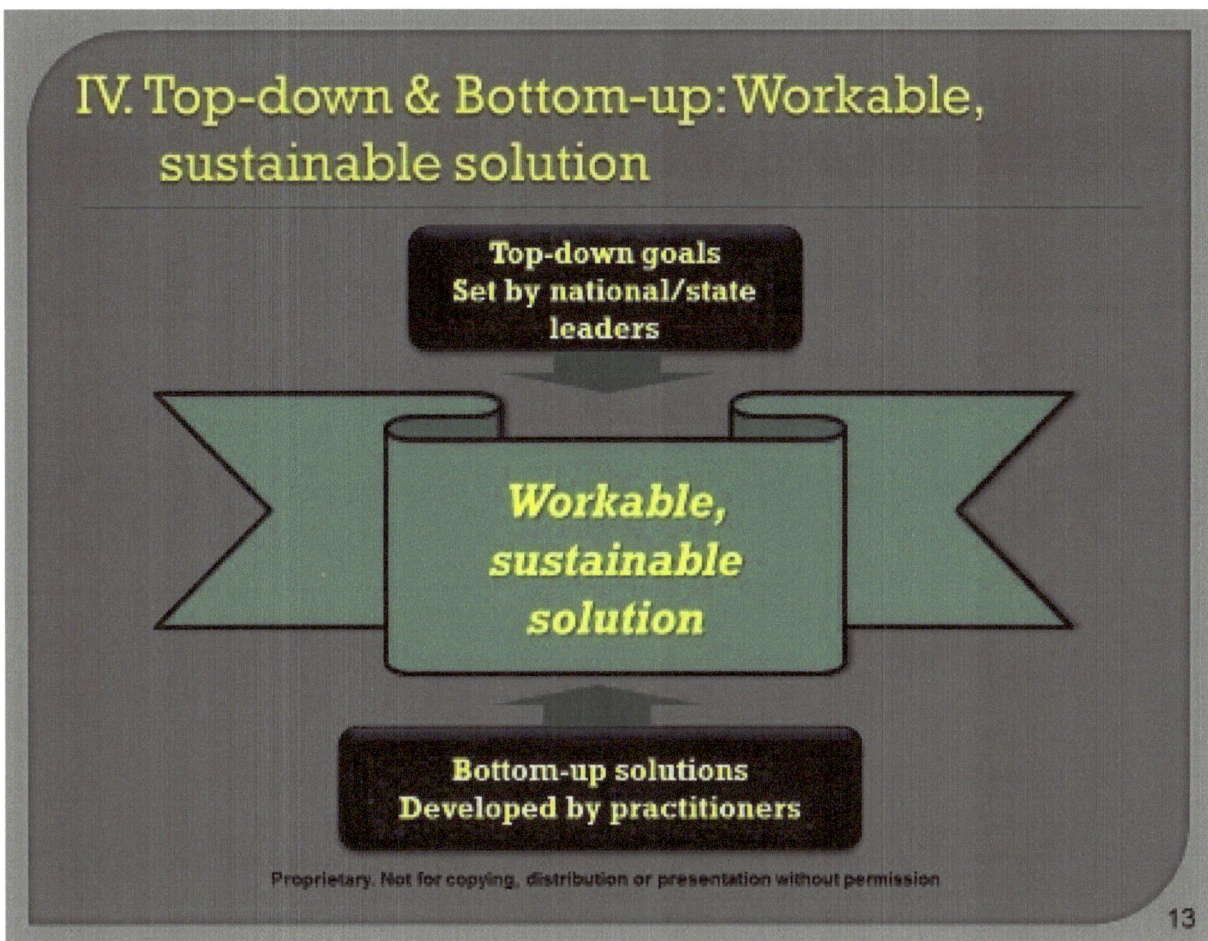

A top-down and bottom-up approach is needed to establish a sustainable solution. Goals set by national and state leaders (top-down) could include percent of GDP or per-capita healthcare costs. Bottom-up solutions are developed by practitioners (payers, providers, and suppliers).

Both top-down and bottom-up approaches need be done consecutively for a workable, sustainable solution. It is inappropriate for senior leadership to decide how things should work from an operational point of view of bottom-up solutions, just as it is inappropriate for practitioners to establish top-down goals.

Simultaneous effort

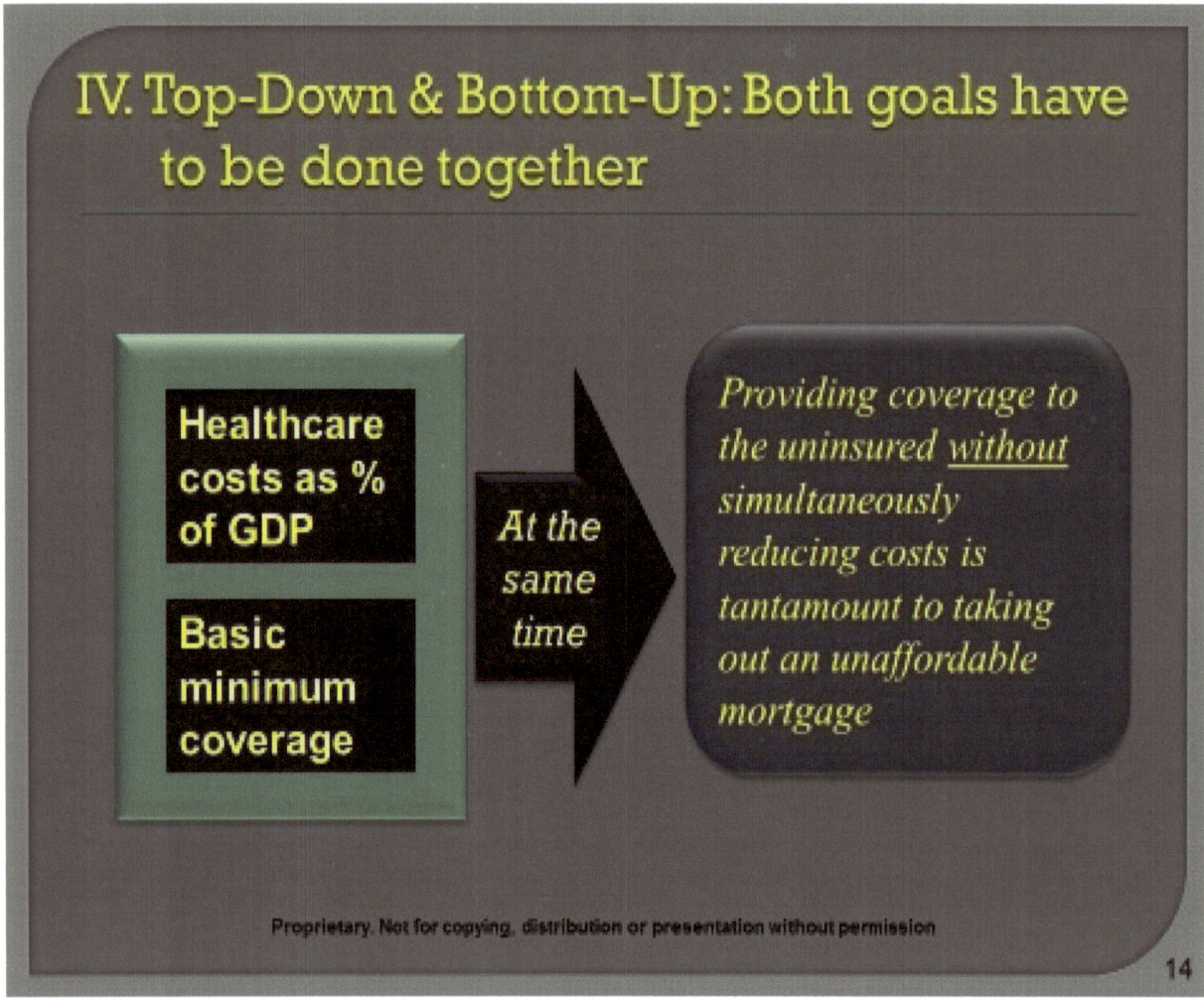

Both approaches have to be done at the same time. We must as a country provide a cap on healthcare costs, either in terms of the percent of GDP or per capita. At the same time, we must provide a goal for basic minimum coverage, which is important for any industrialized nation.

Both goals have to be done at the same time. Why? ***Because providing coverage to the uninsured without simultaneously reducing cost is just like taking out an unaffordable mortgage.***

Recall what happened to the financial services industry: mortgages were being handed out to anybody who wanted them, even though many were not qualified to have mortgages. The outcome was that costs went out of control, and the industry collapsed. Hence, it is imperative that we reduce healthcare costs at the same time as we provide minimum coverage.

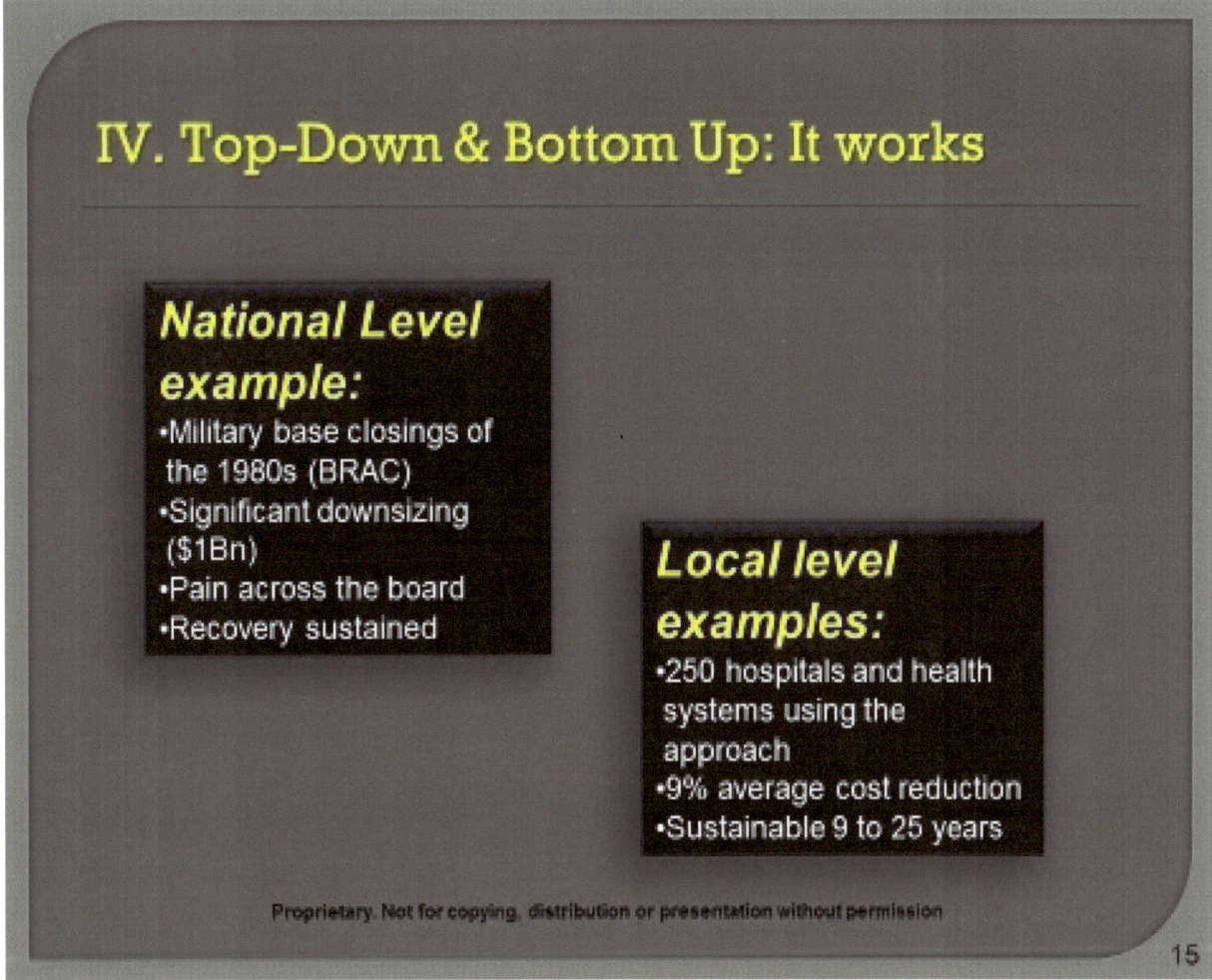

The top-down and bottom-up approach has worked. At the national level, many of you recall the military base closings of the 1980s (BRAC). There was significant downsizing, with a reduction of approximately a billion dollars in annual costs. There was great pain across the board (nobody felt that they were being unfairly targeted), and the result was a more cost-effective and functional system.

At the local level, over 250 hospitals and health systems have used the top-down, bottom-up approach. They have achieved an average annual cost reduction of 9% in operating expenses. The reduction was sustainable, typically, from nine to twenty-five years.

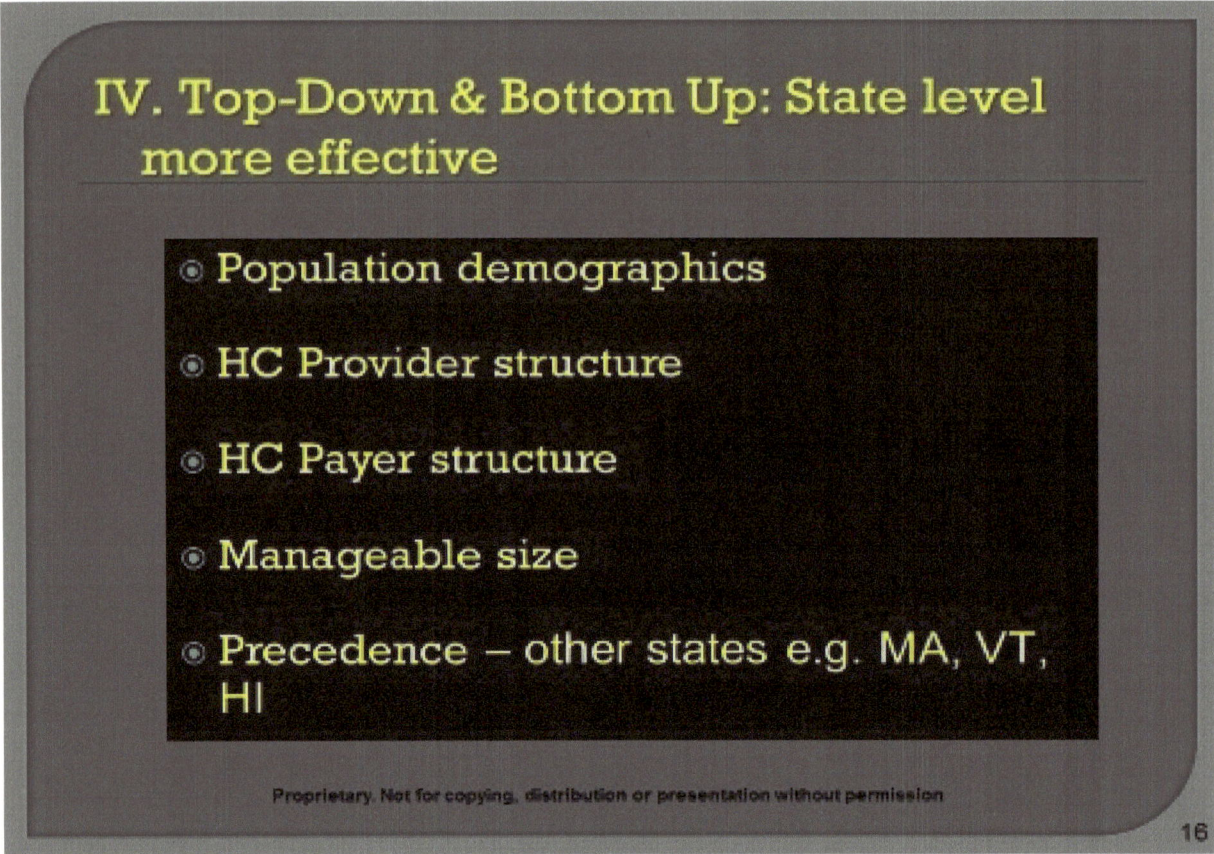

The top-down and bottom-up approach is more effectively undertaken at the state, not federal, level. Population demographics vary by state, and healthcare provider structure in each state also differs, as does the payer structure. This approach is intensive and needs to be undertaken on a manageable size - not for 350 million people, but for 6, 10, or even 30 million people.

There is precedence at the state level; e.g. Massachusetts, Vermont, and Hawaii have undertaken healthcare reform, albeit they did it under a top-down approach, not top-down and bottom-up. Massachusetts undertook its reform in 2006, with a goal of providing basic minimum coverage to everyone. Because no cost target was set at the state level, Massachusetts now has the lowest percent of the uninsured population (under 1%) and the highest per-capita cost healthcare in the U.S. Hawaii undertook healthcare reform a few years ago. The system went bankrupt because the revenue did not meet the costs. Again, this state met the same issue as Massachusetts; costs needed to be reduced at the same time as the provision of minimum coverage. Vermont's healthcare reform occurred too recently (approximately three years ago), thus it is too soon to judge the outcome.

Cost variance by state

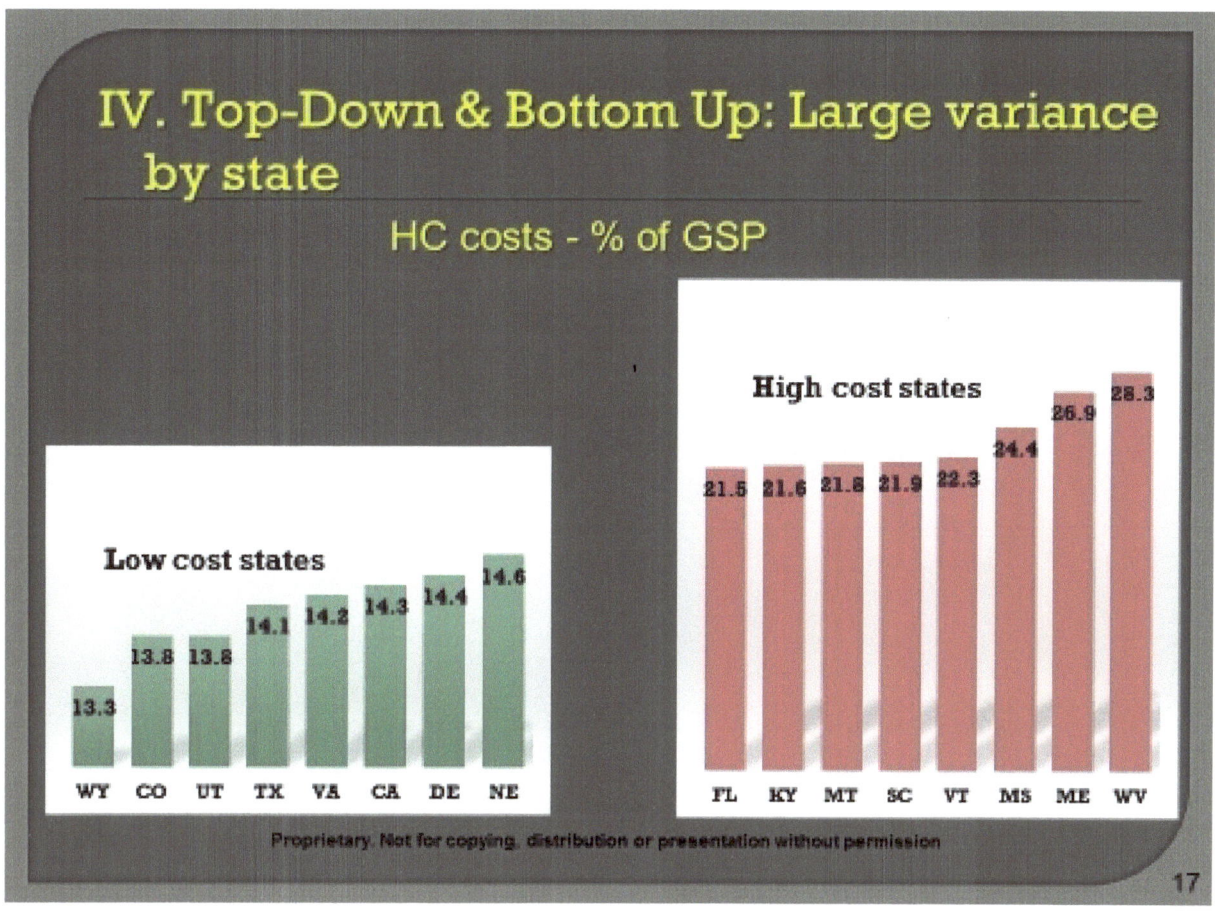

Another indicator that healthcare restructuring needs to be done at the state level, is the large variation in costs. The left-hand chart seen above in green shows the lost-cost states as a percentage of the Gross State Product (GSP) – Wyoming is at 13.3% while Nebraska is at 14.6%,

The red chart on the right shows the high-cost states – from Florida is at 21.5% to West Virginia at 28.3%.

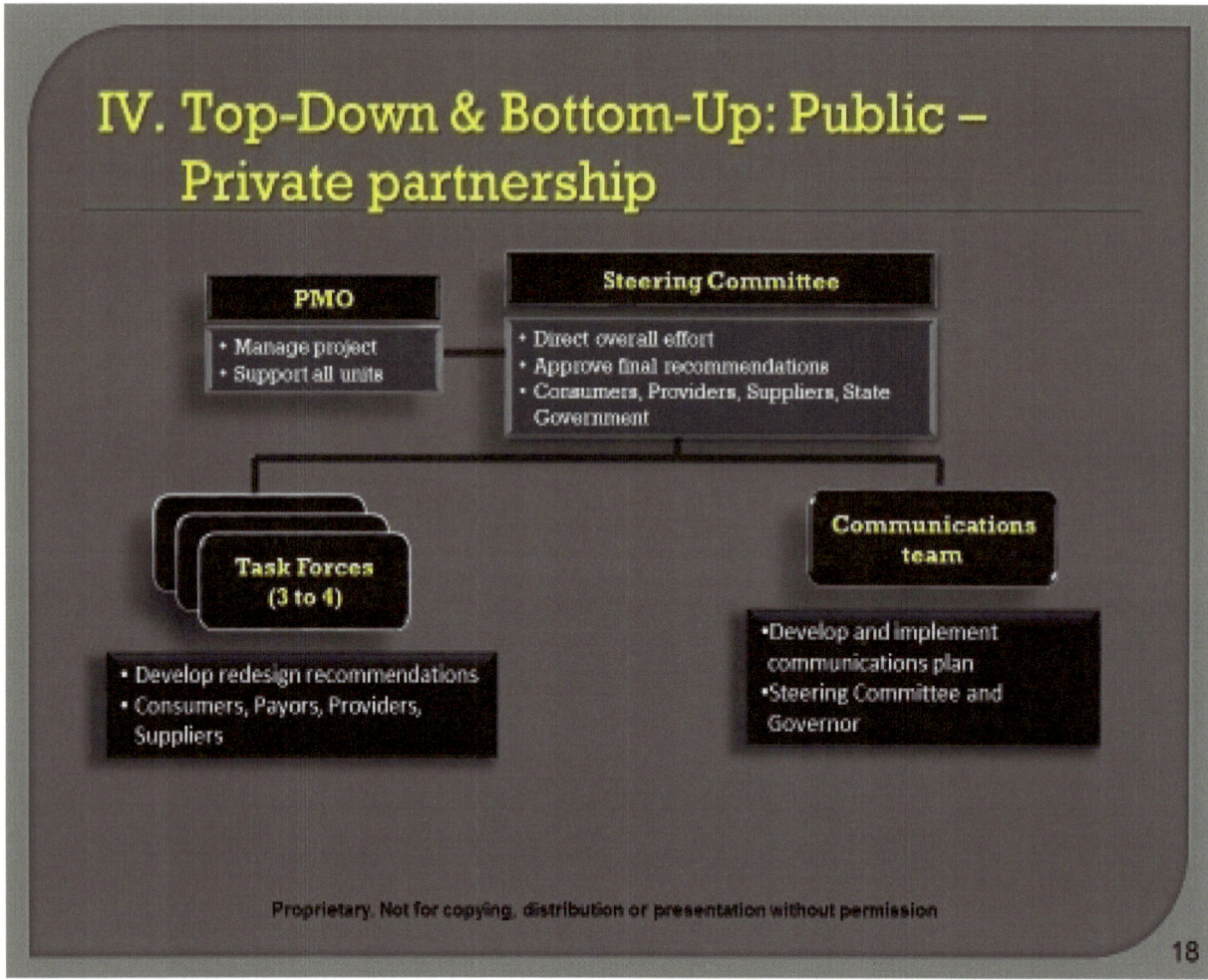

A top-down and bottom-up approach is most effective when there is a public-private partnership. Within this partnership, a steering committee is set up that directs the overall effort. Its members set goals and approve final recommendations. The steering committee should be composed of consumers, providers, suppliers, and the state government.

Within this partnership should also be set up three or four task forces. Each task force may have ten, fifteen, or twenty participants. They develop re-design recommendations for the steering committee's approval. Each task force is composed of consumers, payers, providers, and suppliers.

A project management office should be set up to manage the project and support the steering committee and task forces in their effort. Finally, a communication team should be established to communicate progress and results. This process is very transparent. The communication team has to be proactive to ensure that communications are clear, accurate, and transparent.

Summary

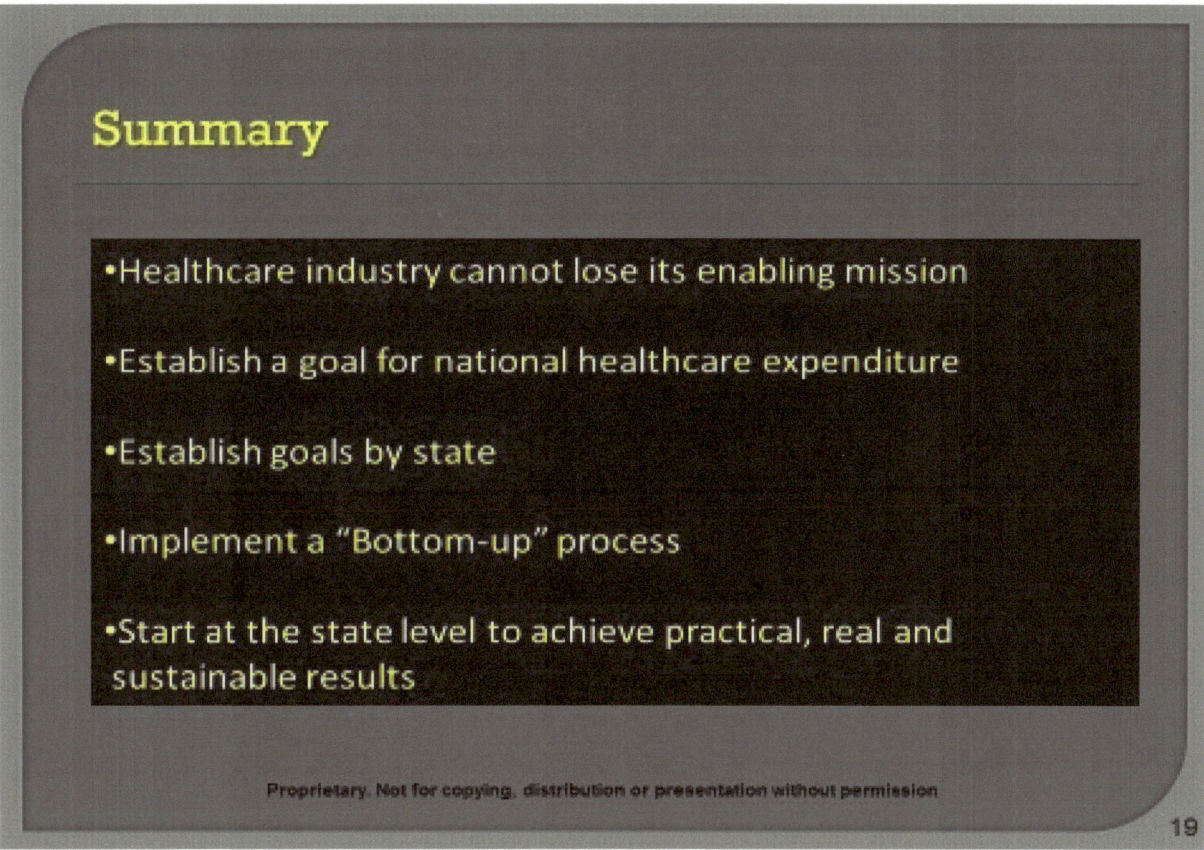

In summary, the healthcare industry cannot lose its enabling mission, because if it does, it will very likely face a major crisis like that of the financial services industry. We need to establish a top-down goal for national healthcare expenditure and minimum basic coverage.

National goals need to be translated into goals for each state. We need to implement a bottom-up process within each state to develop re-design solutions to meet the goals.

Conclusion

If the citizens of the United States were satisfied with their government, there would be no need for this book. Americans would be building, incrementally, on efficiency in the workplace and satisfaction with leadership.

That vision, however, remains a fantasy, farther away than ever as we complete the second decade of the 21st Century. A majority of Americans today (over 60 percent) believe the country is headed in the wrong direction. A greater number (over 80 percent), is of the mind that Congress is not doing its job.

Why the disconnect between the governor and the governed? Where is a relatively young country, under 250 years-old, going wrong? Where is the vigor and enthusiasm of the pioneers? The "can-do" spirit of the founders? The optimistic entrepreneurs? The working-class plying its trade and always learning more at night school? The upwardly-mobile waves of immigrants?

The United States has resigned itself to inhabiting a stagnant malaise when it comes to leadership. Why? Why have we allowed government to play by a set of rules unthinkable in the world of business or even non-profits. The rules that would make any company unresponsive to its own workers and unprofitable for its shareholders are not only tolerated when it comes to government, but often encouraged.

That is bad enough. Worse, in an effort to placate our population, the country's leadership is always in a, "We are doing something," mode, which is often more dangerous than neglect. We must do something, our leaders reason, but they do so without understanding the source of the problem they are seeking to solve.

The result?

We provide solutions that, "put out the fire," that buy time but fail to provide the solutions that deal with roots. In some cases, we merely delay solutions. In many, we exacerbate the problems and make the cost of real resolution much higher and, sometimes, impossible. Confronting structural problems today may be wrenching, but the out-of-sight costs of not acting today may be catastrophic.

Our resignation to accepting mediocrity in government is not inevitable. It is a question of our national willpower. Utilizing "Bottom-up," a proven management approach and its templates, rather than political ones, will turn what some consider "intractable" mediocrity into excellence.

Faith in leadership should be a given, not a question of chance. The depressing statistics cited above should be inverse. The decline in faith in the institution of government is not inevitable.

The "bottom-up" approach rallies key stakeholders around a set of shared values and goals. The shared values and goals help ensure that the majority are "moving in the same direction." This approach is longer, more painful and time-consuming than one mandated or legislated by politicians. However, the results are sustainable. They have real results for those with a stake in the solution.

The, "We know better," approach of politicians, now a mainstay of American government, vanishes once and for all.

Grassroots Metamorphosis offers citizens a path to play their role in recapturing the very essence of our country's creation: self-reliance, independent thinking, faith in the electoral system and sacrifice for the common-good.

If these two questions are answered in the affirmative, there is hope: Are we ready to listen to "bottom-up" management? Once we've listened, are we committed to implementing?

Therein, **Grassroots Metamorphosis.**

Sources of Data

Primary Sources:

- CIA World Factbook
- Organization of Economic Cooperation and Development (OECD)
- Fund for Peace
- Infoplease
- United States Patent and Trademark Office
- Nobel Prize website
- Transparency International
- International Bank for Reconstruction and Development (IBRD – World Bank)
- Freedom House
- Economist Intelligence Unit
- United States Bureau of Economic Analysis
- Office of Management and Budgets
- United States Government Spending
- World Resources Institute
- Reporters without Borders
- Globescan/PIPA
- Cornell Advanced Human Resources Sciences
- Wall Street Journal
- Kaiser Family Foundation
- Manpower Group

Partial list of books and studies

- The Constitution of the United States with All the Amendments, The Declaration of Independence, and the Articles of Confederation – Prepared for publication by Charles F. Stamper
- The Anti-Federalist Papers and the Constitutional Debates – Edited by Ralph Ketcham
- Thomas Jefferson: The Art of Power – Jon Meacham
- Suicide of a Superpower – Patrick Buchanan
- In Search of Excellence – Tom Peters and Robert Waterman
- Execution – The discipline of getting things done – Larry Bossidy and Ram Charan
- Re-engineering the Corporation – Michael Hammer and James Campy
- Corporate Cultures – Terry Deal and Allan Kennedy
- The Wisdom of Teams – Jon R. Katzenbach and Douglas K. Smith
- Redesigning Healthcare Delivery – Peter Boland Editor
- Performance and The Twin Engines of Work – Douglas K. Smith and Sa'ad Allawi

The Author

Sa'ad Allawi has been making the American workplace more productive for 40 years. He has done so by listening and forging consensus among everyone in an organization. He gets *everyone* to, "buy in."

Mr. Allawi has done this job as the co-founder and chairman of the board of Performance Logic Inc. His experience, by a coincidence of time and place, has been primarily in health care, working for NextEra, a consulting firm; chairing the provider practice of William M. Mercer, the world's largest benefits consulting company, and; directing operations improvement practice for APM, a leader in healthcare consulting.

Outside of healthcare, Mr. Allawi, a native of Iraq and mechanical engineer (thermodynamics and nuclear), was the director of business development for AI industries, the largest private Kuwaiti

conglomerate. He worked for McKinsey and Co., the world's premier global management consulting firm, providing services to *Fortune 100* companies and public sector organizations. Earlier, he worked for CA Parsons, a turbine generator manufacturer, and was a section leader for MW Kellogg, petrochemical design-engineers.

Mr. Allawi served on the advisory boards several healthcare, consulting, and technology companies, and advised the Coalition Provisional Authority, or CPA, on private-sector development in Iraq. He is the author of numerous white papers and 20 articles on healthcare management entities including Healthcare Forum, Clinical Laboratories Management Review, Viewpoint (Marsh and McLennan Companies Quarterly), Business Quarterly (University of Western Ontario), Hospital Marketing and Public Relations, and Healthcare Productivity Report.

Mr. Allawi co-authored **100 Top Hospitals,** a study that has become the national benchmark for gauging hospital performance. He authored a chapter of **Redesigning Healthcare Delivery,** by Boland Healthcare, entitled "Applying Performance Engineering to Healthcare Organizations."

Mr. Allawi, past President of a Rotary chapter, received a Bachelor of Engineering in Mechanical Engineering, with concentrations in Thermodynamics and Nuclear, from Liverpool University. He holds an MBA from Columbia University, School of Business, with a specialty in Operations Research and International Business.